PORTFO

THE MARWARIS

THOMAS A. TIMBERG is a scholar and consultant on economic development. His writings cover subjects ranging from Baghdadi Jews in India to contemporary microfinance and Islamic finance. His Harvard doctoral dissertation was on the Marwaris as industrial entrepreneurs, and he has continued to follow the affairs of the members of this community.

GURCHARAN DAS is a world-renowned author, commentator and public intellectual. His bestselling books include *India Unbound*, *The Difficulty of Being Good* and *India Grows at Night*. His other literary works consist of a novel, *A Fine Family*, a book of essays, *The Elephant Paradigm*, and an anthology, *Three Plays*. A graduate of Harvard University, Das was CEO of Procter & Gamble, India, before he took early retirement to become a full-time writer. He lives in Delhi.

THE STORY OF INDIAN BUSINESS
Series Editor: Gurcharan Das

THE STORY OF INDIAN BUSINESS

THE MARWARIS

From Jagat Seth to the Birlas

THOMAS A. TIMBERG

Introduction by
Gurcharan Das

**PORTFOLIO
PENGUIN**

An imprint of Penguin Random House

PORTFOLIO

USA | Canada | UK | Ireland | Australia
New Zealand | India | South Africa | China

Portfolio is part of the Penguin Random House group of companies
whose addresses can be found at global.penguinrandomhouse.com

Published by Penguin Random House India Pvt. Ltd
7th Floor, Infinity Tower C, DLF Cyber City,
Gurgaon 122 002, Haryana, India

Penguin
Random House
India

First published in Allen Lane by Penguin Books India 2014

ISBN 9780143424055

Typeset in Aldine401 BT by Ram Das Lal, New Delhi

Printed at Repro Knowledgecast Limited, India

CONTENTS

LIST OF MAPS

LIST OF FAMILY TREES

ACKNOWLEDGEMENTS

Besides the numerous people who assisted me in my book *The Marwaris*, published in 1978, I wish to thank Gita Piramal, Bimla Poddar, Vaibhav Tulsyan, Shekhar Krishnan, Matthew Rudolph, Medha Kudaisya and, of course, Gurcharan Das for their assistance in updating the material presented here.

INTRODUCTION

'The thrill, believe me, is as much in the battle as in the victory.'

—David Sarnoff, 1891–1971

One sultry evening in 1971, I ran into Tom Timberg in Bombay. I recognized him right away from my days at the university. He was fair and tall, and stood out in the crowd at Chowpatty, his shock of brown hair flying wildly in the strong breeze. He was returning to the US after a year in Rajasthan and Calcutta, having completed research for his PhD dissertation on the rise of Marwari merchants. His enthusiasm was infectious and I took him home, and he found in me a good listener. I was fascinated by his riveting account of how a tiny community from the desert sands of Rajasthan had spread out to every corner of north, east and central India, settling in thousands of villages and towns in the nineteenth century. With their enormous appetite for risk, the Marwaris controlled much of India's inland trade by the end of the First World War. Gradually they turned to industry after the war, and by 1970 they controlled much of the nation's private industrial assets, and by 2011 the Marwaris accounted for a quarter of the Indians on the *Forbes* list of billionaires.

Timberg and I talked late into the night but his account had only reached the 1930s. I was amused at the thought of this irrepressible brown-haired 'yogi' travelling from one district to another in north-west Rajasthan, poring over the commercial records of this quiet and secretive community. I must have ingested a fair amount that evening for I remembered some of his anecdotes when I wrote *India Unbound* a quarter of a century later. The crucial question he posed that night is the same one that hangs over this book: What makes Marwaris so successful? He wrestles with it in a different manner than his earlier work as he brings the Marwari story to date.

Timberg said to me that night that a nation needs many things to succeed economically, but the most important of all is the entrepreneur. An entrepreneur takes great risks when he combines the factors of production—capital, labour and land—with technology. His argument amounted to a challenge to Max Weber's famous thesis, which argued that the industrial revolution did not come to India partly because the traditional Indian businessman lacked the 'Protestant ethic' of thrift, hard work and rationality, which had helped northern European and American businessmen to accumulate capital and exploit the new technology of the steam engine. Timberg claimed that India was equally blessed with the Marwaris, Banias, Jains and other business communities whose work ethic could be as effective as the Protestant's. India required craftsmen, scholars, public servants, but it also needed merchants. The pursuit of *artha*, economic well-being, was the traditional dharma of the Bania. This was not an intuitive idea to the socialist mind of the twentieth century. Thus, Mahatma Gandhi and others had to remind Indians during the freedom struggle about the rightful place of the businessman in nation building. It also became a theme in early-twentieth-century Hindi literature during the freedom struggle when Maithili Sharan Gupt, for example, wrote, 'After "made in India", let India everywhere appear.'

Old and New Prejudices against Money

When I was growing up I knew the Marwari only as the furtive shopkeeper around the corner in villages and towns dotting India. Like the Jew in Europe, he was the last-resort moneylender who charged vicious rates of interest, dispossessing widows of their land and their jewellery when the loan was not repaid. This old prejudice intensified during our 'socialist age', during the first forty years after Independence. It was only after 1991 that our perception of the Marwaris and business people began to change. By and large, the Marwaris have not enjoyed the social status that they have yearned for. My own view changed dramatically when I entered the world of business in Bombay and discovered how much they were revered and even feared for their enormous commercial skills and talent.

A successful merchant has always provoked envy and it is not surprising that the Marwaris have been at the receiving end of resentment and even loathing, especially in Bengal where they achieved their greatest success. Timberg once related the story of a boarding house in Calcutta where he stayed in 1970 at the height of the Naxalite insurgency. Also residing there were two tenants, a Marwari and a Bengali. The Marwari was a heavyset insurance salesman from Bikaner, energetic, enthusiastic and loud. The Bengali tenant, annoyed by his buoyancy, burst out one morning: 'The Naxalites will surely get you one day, you Marwaris!' To which the insurance man replied calmly, 'Before they do, we will join them.' The answer reflected the supple nature of the Marwaris, and indeed of most business communities. Their ability to adapt to situations and a flexibility of mind are surely important traits responsible for their extraordinary success.

When I met Timberg in Bombay in the 1970s, many believed that the Marwaris had been great beneficiaries of the socialist 'Licence Raj'. In fact, R.K. Hazari in his famous Monopolies Inquiry Commission report in 1967 indicted them for having taken advantage of the licensing system by cornering licences, which limited competition in the market. This report led to the dreaded Monopolies and Restrictive Trade Practices (MRTP) Act, which penalized an entrepreneur for producing beyond his licensed capacity—this at a time when the country was starved for the supply of almost everything. I recall at the time that there had been an unprecedented cold wave and sales of Vicks VapoRub, one of the leading products of my company, had risen dramatically. I was warned by our lawyers that we might have to go to jail for 'exceeding our licensed capacity'. Instead of promoting competition, MRTP raised barriers to entry and ended up promoting monopoly. No wonder it is remembered as one of the most oppressive faces of our socialist age.

I primarily disagree with the conclusions of the Hazari commission. I feel that the Marwaris lost out during the forty years of the socialist licensing. Since market share was won in a bureaucrat's office when a licence was acquired, it distorted a businessman's behaviour. Instead of focusing on the market, the businessman applied his talents to managing the government. Competition is the school in which companies learn to perfect their skills. By closing the economy and discouraging competition, socialism made Indian business houses complacent and insensitive to customer needs. They lost the incentive to improve their products and acquire marketing skills. When the economy opened in 1991 and markets became increasingly competitive, the old business houses were suddenly in trouble. They had to relearn business skills and it took them more than a decade to do so.

Timberg in his present volume returns to these themes forty years after his first book on the Marwaris appeared on the stands in the late 1970s, in English and in Hindi. He now inquires whether the Marwaris will continue to play a large role in the future and how they will serve India's development in the twenty-first century. Although Timberg specifically asks this of the Marwaris, one can extend it to India's other traditional business communities. A way to ponder on this is to ask another question—if over sixty countries introduced the same reforms as India did in the early 1990s, why then did India become the world's second-fastest growing economy in the first decade of the twenty-first century? My own hypothesis is that India has been fortunate in having communities who for centuries have known how to conserve and grow their capital. When opportunities arose, they responded. If you set in motion liberal reforms in such a society, you will get a 'bigger bang for your buck', as the Americans put it. This is borne out by the fact that 67 per cent of the Indian billionaires on the *Forbes* list for 2011 had a surname from a traditional business community. This is, of course, politically incorrect thinking, suggesting that our much-reviled caste system might have some redeeming features.

The Virtue of Being Risk-Takers

The business world rewards those who take risks. The incredible achievements of the Marwaris have often been credited to their extraordinary risk-taking ability. 'You don't want to compete against a Marwari!' is the wisdom of the bazaar. G.D. Birla's colossal success in the market for jute futures during the First World War, which laid the foundation for the Birla family's entry into industry, is credited to his phenomenal appetite for risk. Less well known is the remarkable story of Ramkrishna Dalmia, about which he wrote in his book *Some Notes and Reminiscences* in 1948 which he published through the press of the *Times of India*, the famous newspaper that he owned.

Dalmia came from arid Rohtak in Haryana, not far from Rajasthan, the homeland of the Marwaris. Although his great-grandfather was one of the wealthiest men in India, young Dalmia grew up in penury in Calcutta during the 1930s' Depression. Dalmia was twenty-two when his father died and he had to support his mother, grandmother, three sisters and his wife in a single room that he had rented for Rs 13 per month. He was young and adventurous and wanted to get rich quickly. He had speculated in silver and lost and suffered the humiliation of defaulting on his debts. Declared insolvent, he had become persona non grata in the marketplace. He was down and out without a rupee to his name when he received a telegram from London informing him that the market for silver was set to rise.

Dalmia rushed to the bazaar and entreated his friends and associates to buy silver. But he was spurned and laughed at. He next went to a wealthy astrologer, who had predicted that Dalmia would one day grow very rich. The astrologer agreed to purchase silver worth £7500, for which young Dalmia would only earn only Rs 100 as commission. The astrologer also gave him Rs 10 for sending the telegram. Since he did not have the fare for a tonga, Dalmia jumped on to a tram to the general post office and sent off the telegram.

The next day, as he was praying during his daily dip in the Ganga, a messenger came from the astrologer and told him to cancel the transaction. Dalmia was stunned and he rushed to the astrologer and pleaded before him, reminding him of his prophecy, but to no avail. On his return home, he received a telegram confirming the transaction along with the bad news that the market had gone down and that he had lost half the capital the same day. The market, however, turned very quickly in the next few days and since he had not squared his account, he suddenly found that he had made a significant profit. A prudent man would have booked his profit, but Dalmia was a risk-taker. He stole his wife's only ornament and pawned it for Rs 200, and made another bet through another agent for another £10,000. The silver market rose again and he doubled his capital, which he used to buy more silver through a third agent. Soon his profits had risen sevenfold.

Dalmia desperately wanted to unburden himself, and as he was friendless, he confided in his mother. He told her that he had stolen his wife's jewellery. She ordered him to immediately retrieve his wife's ornament from the pawnbroker and never to try and earn again from stolen capital. She also assured him that they could live comfortably on Rs 50 per month. He gave in to his mother's wishes and sent a telegram to his agents to book his profits. But as luck would have it, the telegram got garbled in transmission; the market rose again dramatically, and now his profits were fifteen times his capital, as a consequence of which he had become a very wealthy man. Thus, Dalmia laid the foundations of a vast industrial and real estate empire, and went on to become, as Timberg tells us, one of the three largest industrialists of India. When I was a child, the names 'Tata, Birla, Dalmia' were mentioned in one breath in our home. He was also a bon vivant and had a colourful personal life, with many marriages and passionate affairs.

Dalmia does not explain if he followed any method while speculating. There does not appear to have been an 'art of managing risk' which Timberg speaks about in this volume. He seems to have employed intuition, not unlike George Soros when he bet against the British pound, or the early Rothschilds, the famous Jewish family that financed many kingdoms in Europe. Despite the rationalization that many speculators offer after the fact, the truth is that luck does play a big part in the markets for commodity futures. Hence, Dalmia comes out sounding like a gambler at heart, not unlike the famous Yudhishthira, the 'unhero' of the Mahabharata.

Trust Is at the Heart of It

One of the lessons of Dalmia's story is that trust has a central place in business life. When Dalmia defaulted on his debt, he broke a promise, and the market punished him swiftly. By losing the trust of his peers in the market he turned from a somebody to a nobody, a terrible thing to happen to any human being. William James, the American philosopher, explained in his classic, *The Principles of Psychology*, that

> no more fiendish punishment could be devised than that one should be turned loose in society and remain absolutely unnoticed . . . If no one turned around when we entered, answered when we spoke, or minded what we did, but if every person we met 'cut us dead' and acted as if we were non-existent things, a kind of rage and impotent despair would ere long well up in us.

The fact is that our self-worth is held hostage to the opinion of others, and while we may not admit it, the truth is that we all seek to be 'somebody'.

In the world of Marwaris and Banias the word for trust is *sakh* and it is linked closely to honour. It is a crucial indicator of a merchant's standing. Sakh is at the heart of creditworthiness and business integrity and means much more than wealth and financial strength. It is acquired through an unblemished record in honouring obligations, being generous to the needy and having a philanthropic outlook. The cotton trader Ramvilas Poddar began as a humble *dalal* or broker in the raw-cotton trade but soon reached an eminent position in the bazaar by quickly building a reputation for honesty and acquiring sakh within the community. This helped Poddar set up an independent brokerage and encouraged older and established firms to entrust their money to a newcomer in the bazaar.

G.D. Birla, who established the great Birla fortune as we have just mentioned, confirms the importance of sakh. In describing Birla's life as a jute trader, Medha Kudaisya tells us that most of his transactions in buying raw jute or selling the finished product were based on the trader's word. The commodity fluctuated on a daily basis and there were often great swings in price between morning and evening. Sellers and brokers presented their offers on a rough sheet of paper in the morning but the mills took their decision in the evening. The offers were invariably honoured, no matter how the market fared during the day.

My friend Raju Kanoria, who also started his life in the

jute business and went on to become a president of FICCI,
the prestigious chambers of commerce, corroborates
that at the East India Jute & Hessian Exchange prices
were confirmed on a handshake. He went on to add that
a similar system based on trust operated in the case of
finished stock. The jute mills held finished goods in stock
for buyers against Pucca Delivery Orders made months
in advance and the mills never dared to default on them.
When Kanoria was eighteen he had the good fortune to
meet G.D. Birla whose only advice to young Kanoria was
'to trust people if you want to succeed'.

The visible embodiment of sakh is the negotiable
financial instrument called Hundi. A centuries-old Bania
innovation, the Hundi was akin to a bill of exchange
which allowed a merchant in a remote village to remit
or receive large sums of money on the basis of trust.
For instance, a merchant from remote Gujarat, after
selling his raw cotton in Bombay, could minimize risk
by receiving a Hundi in lieu of cash. Instead of receiving
payment in cash with all its inherent risks during transit,
he would take a Hundi for the equivalent amount drawn
by the buyer in his favour. The Hundi entitled him to
present it to an agent in his village and collect his money
there. This made it possible to transfer funds without
having to physically transact in cash. While the Hundi
began as a remittance facility, it evolved over time as a

credit instrument which the holder could use to take a loan. The lender extended the loan amount at a discount on the value of the Hundi and subsequently encashed it at par. In sum, the Hundi became a negotiable instrument.

Those who are overly enthusiastic about regulating the market, and even before they think about a new law and a new regulator, ought to remember that there are self-regulating mechanisms within the market, such as sakh, that keep bad behaviour in check. The market itself is neither moral nor immoral but it does tend to reward good actions and punish bad ones. A businessman who treats his customers, suppliers and employees fairly will be trusted by the market, and this in turn will build reputation and market share.

At the heart of the market system is the trust between self-interested strangers who come together to exchange in the marketplace. The reason that buyers and sellers are able to trust each other in the market is, in part, due to the underlying belief that the average person acts honestly—that he or she wants to do the right thing—and this gives people a sense of safety when they transact. This is why a seller readily accepts a cheque from a buyer. Millions of transactions in the global economy are conducted daily based on trust, without resorting to contracts. The market depends ultimately not on laws but on the self-restraint of individuals. However, the market also fails, and it is often unable to discipline the dishonest. Hence the need for laws and regulations, and the enforcement machinery. However, a good state rules with a light touch that causes the least discomfort to the honest everyday person.

The Footprint of the Owner is the Best Fertilizer

Timberg has highlighted the reasons for the success of Marwari firms. However, it is important to understand why some of the Great Firms declined and fell, including perhaps the greatest of the Great Firms, Tarachand Ghanshyam Das, which closed in 1957. Timberg has written much about this firm, and rightly so, with enthusiasm. It enjoyed such prestige and credibility that its Hundi was negotiable through multiple offices and accepted by moneylenders and traders across the country. The great Birla family got its start in Calcutta as subagents to this firm.

Why did this firm die? I posed this question to my friend Suresh Neotia, whose *nana* (maternal grandfather), Janki Prasad Poddar, was one of the last generation of six brothers who owned the company. Neotia replied that none of the brothers did an honest day's work. They felt that it would diminish their status if they were seen sitting on the *gaddi* in Calcutta's Burra Bazaar, home to the Marwari businessman. A gaddi is literally a large mattress covered with *chandni*, 'white cloth', where the seth, or merchant, parked himself in the morning after his daily puja. Beside him sat his *munim*, bookkeeper and trusted adviser. Gaddi in time came to mean a firm's office and even the firm itself.

When you have money for more than a hundred years in the family, the appetite to make more diminishes. When experienced and trustworthy munims carry on the business independently and successfully, the sensible thing is to delegate and leave them alone. The Poddar seths thus left the running of the business to munims, who had over generations also accumulated shares in the firm and had become junior partners. When the munims tell you that the esteem of the firm will be diminished if the seth sits daily on the gaddi at Mullick Street, you believe them and you go away on a perpetual holiday to Mussoorie.

Sensible, one would think. This is how corporate capitalism has evolved around the world, as owners in the countries where capitalism has matured have gradually left the running of day-to-day business to professional CEOs, who like the munims of old have become millionaires in their own right. The catch, however, is corporate governance. Even the best-managed companies have vigilant boards on which owners often sit, and to which the CEO and the professional managers are accountable. It was different in the case of the Poddar seths, however. As they bought grand bungalows and began to behave like Bengali zamindars, they forgot that the 'footprint of the owner is the best fertilizer'. They ignored their function of governance and not surprisingly the business died slowly.

The Story of Indian Business

The reasons for the success and failure of business enterprise are the sort of issues which engage the authors of our unique multi-volume history of Indian business. *The Marwaris* is the sixth volume in Penguin's The Story of Indian Business series, which mines great ideas in business and economics that have shaped commerce in the Indian subcontinent, while entertaining us with the romance of the high seas and the adventure in the bazaar. Leading contemporary scholars closely examine historical texts, inscriptions and records, and interpret them in a lively, sharp and authoritative manner for the intelligent reader who may not have prior knowledge in these areas. Each slender volume offers an enduring perspective on business enterprise in the past, avoiding the pitfall of simplistically cataloguing a set of lessons for today. The value of the exercise, if we are successful, will be in promoting a longer-term sensitivity in the reader, which can help to understand the material bases for our present human condition and to think sensibly about our economic future. Taken together, the series as a whole celebrates the ideal captured in the Sanskrit word 'artha'.

The series began with Tom Trautmann's interpretation for our times of the renowned treatise on the science of wealth, *Arthashastra*, which was authored over two thousand years ago and is considered the world's first manual on political economy. Kanakalatha Mukund took us to south India in the next volume, *The World of the Tamil Merchant*, to a beguiling world when a ship from Rome would touch one of the ports in south India daily and the Roman senator and writer, Pliny the Elder, called India 'the sink of the world's precious metal' in 77 CE. Mukund has reconstructed this world by drawing on the epics *Silappadikaram* and *Manimekalai* and other historical materials to the end of the Chola Empire. Next, we jumped centuries to Tirthankar Roy's radiant account of the East India Company, which taught us, among other things, how much the modern multinational corporation is a child of a company that is reviled even today in India. Our fourth volume hopped again to the late eighteenth century during the decline of Surat and the rise of Bombay, where Lakshmi Subramanian set the stage for the ups and downs in the adventurous lives of *Three Merchants of Bombay: Trawadi Arjunji Nathji, Jamsetjee Jeejeebhoy and Premchand Roychand*. Arshia Sattar recounts in the fifth volume the brilliant adventures of *The Mouse Merchant* and other tales based on the *Kathasaritsagara*, *Panchatantra* and other mythological sources.

In the future lies a veritable feast. Three more books will cover the ancient and early medieval periods: Gregory Schopen will present the *Business Model of Early Buddhist Monasticism* based on the *Mulasarvastivada Vinaya*; Donald Davis will raise contemporary issues in the area of commercial and business law based on medieval commentaries by authors such as Vachaspati Mishra and Chandeshvara on the voluminous *Dharmashastras*. Scott Levi will take us from the early modern period to the modern one with the over five-hundred-year-old saga of Multani traders in caravans through central Asia, rooted in the works of Zia al-Din Barani (*Tarikh-i-Firuz Shahi*) and Jean-Baptiste Tavernier. The celebrated Sanjay Subrahmanyam and Muzaffar Alam will next transport us into the world of sultans, shopkeepers and portfolio capitalists in Mughal India. Raman Mahadevan will describe the Nattukottai Chettiars' search for fortune. Finally, Medha Kudaisiya will round off the series by breathing life into the debates surrounding the 'Bombay Plan', a fifteen-year economic plan for India, drawn up by eminent industrialists in 1944–45, who wrestled with the idea of proper roles for the public and private sectors.

The privilege of reading these rich and diverse volumes as they come from the pens of our scholars has left me with a sense of wonder at the vivid, dynamic and illustrious role played by trade and economic enterprise in advancing Indian civilization.

Gurcharan Das

Marwari Presence in India

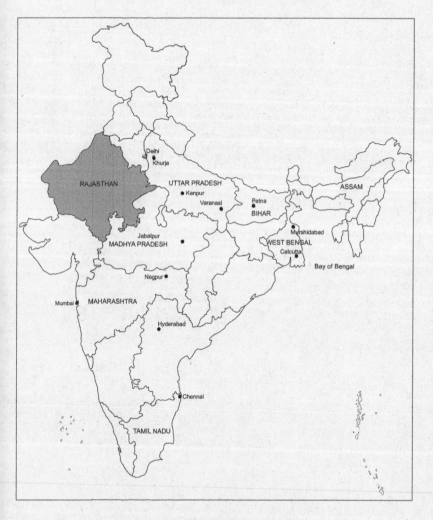

Not to scale

1. PREFACE

Business Communities: Who Are the Marwaris and What Is Their Historical Legacy?

MANY OF THE large family business groups that are prominent in India today come from traditional business families belonging to communities such as the Marwaris, Parsees and Gujaratis. These 'communities' do not comprise Hindu castes precisely, just as their Muslim, Christian or Zoroastrian counterparts too do not. Rather, business communities are groups of castes with a common regional origin and a traditional involvement in trade. Their names typically indicate geographical or in some cases linguistic origin (for example, Gujarati, Punjabi, Marwari, Sindhi).

As K.K. Birla, an erstwhile leading member of the G.D. Birla business family had put it, 'We were born into a family of businessmen, and finance was in our blood, just as chivalry is in the blood of a Rajput, Maratha, Gurkha, Sikh or Jat.'[1] In common parlance, business communities are counterpoised by 'service communities', which typically entered the civil service, professions and academia under the Mughals, the British and in independent India, and are now prominent in the professional executive class. Among the Sindhis, this division is marked by the difference between 'Amils' (civil servants) and 'Bhaibands' (merchants).[2] Most Hindu Sindhis today, whether Amil or Bhaiband, belong to the same caste, the Lohana, but the key distinguishing factor is their 'vocational orientation'. There are certain other Sindhi castes but they are not very significant as a proportion of the community. The differentiation between Amil and Bhaiband emerged quite late within the Lohana caste, and in fact the two groups intermarry and are themselves highly stratified in terms of wealth and social position. Among most non-Sindhi Hindus and for that matter among Muslims too, these business communities are *jati*s or caste-like groups of one sort or another, or sometimes congeries of castes that come from a specific region.

The difference between business and service communities exists in many regions of India. There is both a cultural juxtaposition and sometimes an ethnic one. Children from the business class in Kolkata usually attend St Xavier's College on Park Street in the old European south Kolkata, while those from the service class favour Presidency College on College Street in the Bengali north Kolkata. Similar sets of schools with service- and business-community orientation exist in several major Indian cities. In Mumbai, for instance, there is a divide between those who go to Elphinstone and those who go to St Xavier's, though it is not as marked as it is in Kolkata. In Ahmedabad, the businessmen often send their children to Shreyas while service-class families might patronize institutions which are more Anglo-Indian in orientation.

However, just because some family business groups are owned by families from business communities it does not mean that all of them are. In recent years the net of business entrepreneurship has widened. The descendants of senior civil servants are more likely to be vigorous MBA businessmen than be in the civil service. Harish Damodaran demarcates three paths to successful entrepreneurship in India: the first, from 'markets' for traditional traders; the second, from the 'office' for traditional service classes; and the third, from the 'fields' for traditional farming communities. But he concedes that in north India and for north Indian groups it is the first path, from markets to modern entrepreneurship, that has predominated.[3]

If we are to look up 'Marwari' on Wikipedia we will find a number of references to Marwari horses (a breed), the Marwari language, and Marudesh, the dry and desert areas of western Rajasthan. However, it is generally the traditional merchants from these areas that are designated as 'Marwari'. James Tod, the iconic early-nineteenth-century English historian of Rajasthan, identifies 128 merchant castes with members in Rajasthan—most of these have branches in regions outside Rajasthan as well. In Rajasthan, it is especially the members of the Aggarwal, Maheshwari and Oswal Hindu castes who are prominent. [4] James Tod goes on to say, 'Nine-tenths of the bankers and commercial men of India are natives of Maroo des [Marwar] and these chiefly of the Jain faith.' Though this may have been an exaggeration, the prominence of the Marwaris was apparent even in the early nineteenth century. It has also been seen that the Aggarwals are the more prominent community than the Maheshwaris. There are also other prominent non-Marwari business communities, such as the Gujaratis and Punjabis.

The geographic designation 'Marwari' is often applied to those who come from the broader north Indian area, even if they are not from Marwar precisely. Leading Marwari entrepreneurs today actually come from Shekhawati, a region loosely connected with the old princely state of Jaipur, situated between Delhi and Jaipur, rather than from Jodhpur, Bikaner or Jaisalmer, the classic Marwar. It has been noticed that the numerous Hindi-speaking business-community members from Haryana and Uttar Pradesh are often referred to as 'Marwaris', though the Marwaris from Rajasthan reject this identification and the said members are not welcomed in Marwari organizations.

Though the Marwaris as a community and Marwari firms have dominated the 'bazaar' economy of north India for centuries, their activities were originally focused in their Rajasthan homeland. Later, one group of Marwaris moved east with the Mughals and established business headquarters along the Ganga–Jamuna valley as also in Bengal, which is epitomized by the Jagat Seths and the Varanasi Aggarwals, whom we shall discuss a little later. The Marwari business community established a huge commercial presence especially in eastern and central India, where it displaced various competing trading groups in the nineteenth century—in particular, the Bengali traders in Bengal and, to a lesser extent, the Punjabi Khatris. Not only did the Marwaris achieve considerable standing in commerce in these regions, being Hindi speaking they played a leading role in the revival of Hindi as a language, Hinduism as a modern religion, and the Indian nationalist movement. With their economic resources, they could not but create an impact in all these areas. Even today a large number of Marwaris are prominent in national politics and cultural patronage.[5]

Business communities constitute a small portion of India's population. They are estimated to constitute less than 6 per cent of India's population, and the ones which are particularly successful, far lesser.[6] There are perhaps 3 lakh Marwaris from the Hindu trading castes scattered around India.[7]

With a homeland that is dry and the locus of traditional overland caravan routes, it is not surprising that the Marwaris had spread throughout the country to areas that experienced more rapid commercial growth in the nineteenth century, especially to those regions where competing trading groups were less organized and capital scarce. But it is in Calcutta and the hinterlands of eastern and central India that they were the most prominent.

Each of the subregions of Rajasthan has a different history and its migrants followed somewhat different trajectories in their dispersion. The Shekhawati towns of Fatehpur, Jhunjhunu and Singhana were ruled until the eighteenth century by the Muslim Qaimkhani Nawabs, Rajputs who had been converted to Islam. It is for this reason that many Marwaris bear the names 'Jhunjhunwala' and 'Singhania' though some hail more recently from other Shekhawati towns. Banking business families like the Aggarwal Choudhris of Fatehpur and the Poddars of Ramgarh were associated with these Muslim rulers. In the early eighteenth century, the Qaimkhanis were conquered by various Hindu Shekhawati Rajputs, especially those who made their headquarters in Sikar and Jhunjhunu. The Jhunjhunu rulers followed the normal Rajput practice of dividing their estates amongst their sons, which resulted in a large number of small states and in Jhunjhunu quickly ceasing to be an important destination, except for the popular Rani Sati temple. The fragmentation of estates drove many estate holders to banditry, and the lawlessness of the area was a major factor that led to the migration of merchants. But the numerous small and often financially strapped Shekhawati rulers were also in need of financial services, which only the Marwaris could provide, and this was a pull factor which drew Marwari businessmen. Each small ruler, 'thakur', tried to attract businessmen and needed the financial services of an estate banker—or perhaps more than one. Unusually, the Sikar estate was not partitioned but inherited as a whole by a single heir and thus its rulers were able to promote several towns such as Churu and Ramgarh, which attracted businessmen.

Shekhawati Region

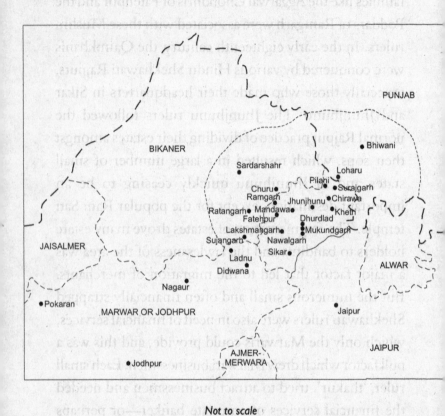

PUNJAB

BIKANER

Bhiwani

Sardarshahr

Loharu

Churu

Pilahi

Surajgarh

Ramgarh

Jhunjhunu

Chirawa

Ratangarh

Mandawa

Khetri

Fatehpur

Dhurdlad

Lakshmangarh

Mukundgarh

JAISALMER

Sujangarh

Nawalgarh

Ladnu

Sikar

ALWAR

Didwana

Nagaur

• Pokaran

Jaipur

MARWAR OR JODHPUR

JAIPUR

AJMER-
MERWARA

• Jodhpur

Not to scale

Jhunjhunu District

Churu

Beri
Likua
Kaji

HARYANA

Dulpura
Malsisar
Asisar
Kakreu Kalan
Dabri
Dhanuri
Bissau
Churela
Lutu
Luna
Toliyasar
Mojas
Lumas
Bhojasar
Jejusar
Satwara
Chelsi
Kumawas

Pilani
Ghumansar
Lamba
Budana
Kalipahari

JHUNJHUNU

Nua
Bakra
Susuab
Basawa
Ker
Gudha
Nawalgarh
Ponkh

Dulaniya
Bhaothari
Kasni
Jakhod
Asalwas
Deorod
Kakoda
Dhulwa
Chirawa
Buhana
Panthroli
Gadanian
Sultana
Mainana
Pacheri
Raipur
Ghardana
Indali
Singhana
Salana
Gowla
Fatehpura
Khetri
Papurna
Gadrata
Sihore

Raghunathpura
Sikar
Gothra
Jhajhar
Mahanbari
Chirana
Udaipurwati

Not to scale

Despite their occasional oppression of merchants, the various Shekhawati rulers competed to get merchants to move to their territories. This competition often took the form of tax exemptions, including the exemption of octroi, a duty on the intercity transport of goods. Anand Yang in his study of markets in northern Bihar details the extent to which the big Bihari zamindars bid for prosperous merchants, including the Marwaris, to strengthen the market centres under their jurisdiction.[8] This process is similar to how European rulers competed to get rich businessmen to settle in their realms throughout the feudal period.

S.N. Tewari in his book *Business Communities and the Freedom Struggle*, focusing on the political role of Marwari businessmen, cites the decline in opportunities available to the rulers of the small princely states of Rajasthan as they started to serve as financiers after they joined the British in establishing peace and order, which thereby lessened the need for them to finance military ventures. This became an impelling factor for the Marwaris to migrate in the eighteenth and nineteenth centuries.[9]

However, Marwari merchants spread across India were sources of revenue for these thakurs. One Shekhawati thakur reported that his father, during his annual trips to Bombay and Calcutta, would collect donations or 'nazarana' from merchants who were originally from his estate or *thikana*. In reverse, migrant merchants sometimes financed the nationalist movement in their home thikanas, in opposition to local rulers. The Birlas took this practice to its logical conclusion by purchasing the estate of their home village, Pilani, from its thakurs. In contemporary Rajasthan politics as well, migrant merchants contribute funds and run for office, both for and against political groups supported by various former feudal rulers and their opponents.

Princely rulers devoted considerable attention to attracting rich merchants, as did their counterparts in other parts of the world. In fact, their activities would be considered standard in any area trying to promote its economic development. The Switzerland or Singapore strategy for promoting development, at least part of it, is providing a safe haven in a hostile region. It was not only Indian businessmen who operated in British India but also the Sassoons from Baghdad, and the Aga Khans from Persia who fled to Bombay because of their precarious situation as minority-community merchants in the Persian Gulf region. They found India to be a good place to run their businesses—just as today some businessmen prefer to work out of Dubai and Bahrain at the one end of the South Asia region, and Singapore and Hong Kong at the other end, to circumvent government regulations and taxation laws. If such businessmen are not fleeing turmoil and disquiet today, they are searching for a more propitious place from where to do business, for reasons of tax, infrastructure or business environment as the jargon now has it.

*

Shekhawati continues to be a backwater and off the beaten path, though Rajasthan has recently participated in the renewed economic growth of Shining India; migrant Marwari business groups and non-Marwari groups as well have participated in the 'shining' of contemporary Rajasthan. The Punjab Haryana Delhi Chamber of Commerce informs us that Rajasthan's income grew annually on an average by 7.4 per cent between 2004 and 2011 and it was considered among India's fastest-growing states. However, Rajasthan is still ranked twelfth among India's states in terms of GDP per capita. Of course, the heavy investments by large Marwari groups are in areas where the economy dictates they should be—big cities, near natural resources and so forth—and not necessarily in the owners' former home villages. Churu and Jhunjhunu were still reported as India's dirtiest cities in a recent 'National Policy Exercise'.[10]

Despite their general backwardness, Shekhawati towns have benefited from their historic role. For centuries, these towns have been home to successful

businessmen—this is evidenced by the enormous
empty palaces or 'havelis' that they had built there,
which because of their elaborate wall murals have now
become places of pilgrimage for those interested in the
art and architecture they represent.[11] Amar Nath and F.
Wacziarg, in *Rajasthan: The Painted Walls of Shekhavati*,
document these havelis at length. The authors of
this book have created a chain of non-hotel hotels,
'Neemrana', which includes the havelis of the Piramals
in Bagar as one of its high points. Wikipedia carries
references to havelis located in other small Rajasthani
towns such as Ramgarh, Fatehpur and Churu. Several
old merchant havelis now offer themselves as heritage
hotels for those who wish to taste what life was at home
for earlier generations of wealthy merchants. There
is a write-up[12] on a Welcome Group hotel in Phalodi
which belonged to the Dadda bankers who came from
that place. The travelogue informs us that the haveli
has been 'lovingly restored' by a current descendant
and even comes with a neighbouring jewellery shop
owned by the hereditary jewellers to the Daddas, now
based in Chennai, who retain an outpost at their home
in Phalodi. In this transformation of merchant havelis
we see a similarity, though on a much larger scale, with
Rajput aristocrats turning their palaces into heritage
hotels. Not only did the migrant merchants build

mansions, they also set up schools, hospitals, wells and tanks, and other public facilities.[13]

After more than a hundred years of migration to Calcutta and other destinations, in many instances young Marwaris have never been to Rajasthan, let alone their traditional home villages, and a number of mansions lie abandoned. However, many families still retain their roots in Rajasthan by maintaining their havelis and the temples and charities connected with them. The Birlas are reported to have family records going back to the nineteenth century at their Pilani haveli. They have set up a large educational complex there, centred around the well-known Birla Institute of Technology & Science, a leading technological university.

Apart from the Shekhawatis, there are important groups of businessmen who hail from the neighbouring areas of western Rajasthan such as Bikaner, Jodhpur and Bhiwani (now in Haryana). The steel magnates, the Mittals for example, come from Sadulpur in Bikaner. 'Mittal' is an Aggarwal subcaste or 'gotra' name and common to several prominent business communities, Marwari and non-Marwari. The Mittals who own the giant telephone company are apparently Punjabis. The same is the case with the Jindals, another prominent steel family. As was observed, the Jagat Seths came from Jodhpur state, and among the large banking families, the

Daddas from Phalodi, the Dagas from Bikaner and the
Malpanis from Jaisalmer.

Western Rajasthan

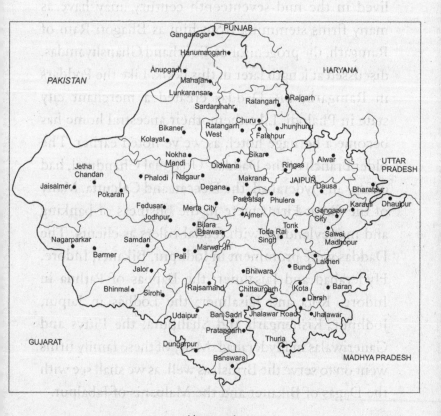

Not to scale

There were a large number of old Great Firms with their origins in Rajasthan which gave rise to many successor firms. Most Marwaris are both related to, and have families who were involved with, these firms. Sargandhas Dadda of Phalodi in Jodhpur, who lived in the mid-seventeenth century, may have as many firms stemming from him as Bhagoti Ram of Ramgarh, the progenitor of Tarachand Ghanshyamdas, discussed at length later in this book. Like the Poddars in Ramgarh, the Daddas created a merchant city state in Phalodi. Like them, their ancestral home has become a heritage hotel, as we've noted earlier. The older branch of the Daddas, Udaymal Chandmal, had offices in Hyderabad, the Deccan and Calcutta. Many of the Great Firms were in the business of banking and moneylending with feudal rulers as clients. The Daddas were prominent in Jodhpur, Bikaner, Indore, Hyderabad and Jaisalmer; the Bapnas of Pathua in Indore, Kota and Jaisalmer; the Lodhas in Jaipur, Jodhpur, Kishengarh and Shahpura; the Pittys and Ganeriwalas in Hyderabad. Many of these family firms went on to serve the British as well, as we shall see with the Dagas of Bikaner and the Malpanis of Jabalpur.

*

Merchant families were amorphous and physically

mobile. Sadulpur, from where the Mittals came, was only settled by migrants from elsewhere in the last two centuries. Everybody came from somewhere and went somewhere else. Their names indicate their places of origin. Just as European Jews with names like Wiener (Vienna), Berliner, Krakauer, Frankfurter, Hamburger, Wilner (Vilna), and others signifying more obscure places typically lived somewhere else in Europe, Marwaris too with names like Jhunjhunwala, Singhania, Jaipuria and so forth had moved from those places to somewhere else. In the name-town itself, the names do not serve to differentiate their bearers from everyone else in the town. Other Marwari names refer to ancestors. The Jalans and Tulsians are descended from the brothers connected with the founding of the Rani Sati temple in Jhunjhunu.[14]

2. THE BEGINNING OF THE BAZAAR ECONOMY

HISTORIANS OF MEDIEVAL and ancient India have documented large-scale transportation of goods by merchants over long distances. These merchants did not only finance trade but also funded states and kings, and in general operated in a long-distance, large-scale 'bazaar' economy.

Rajat Ray explains that there were three levels, as he describes them, in the emerging world economy of the nineteenth century. These were: the metropolitan economy, the local economies, and the 'bazaar' economy.[1] The bazaar economy was a phenomenon which existed independently of the colonial metropoles and the local economy but operated in both. The bazaar economy handled the internal flow of goods across the Indian Ocean and the Bay of Bengal, as also the long-distance transportation of goods and commodities in India. This could include horses from Arabia, pearls from the Persian Gulf, slaves from Africa, opium and cloth from India, and tea and silk from China, as well as to-and-fro transit from Europe. The denizens of the bazaar economy were members of those family firms and business communities that had the necessary commercial systems and tools such as accounting, financial and insurance services, and the logistics to manage the flow of goods. Often, the indigenous people from an area did not have the required skill and acumen which other, often non-European, firms had.

The international bazaar economy was staffed by Baghdadi Jews, Gujarati Hindus and Muslims, Armenians, Greeks, Iranians, Chinese and Portuguese; traditionally the Marwaris limited their involvement to the flow of goods within India.

★

From the sixteenth century onwards, there was an increasing number of European merchants entering the Indian economy, and thereby interacting with the bazaar economy. Portuguese, Dutch, French and, finally dominating the scene, English merchants, in particular the East India Company, made their presence felt. They found various partners in the bazaar economy and among these were some Marwaris. The Marwari Jagat Seths constituted a critical part of this bazaar economy.

The Jagat Seths and the early Aggarwals of Varanasi are reported to have arrived in the trail of the Mughal armies in the seventeenth century. The Jagat Seths and most of their contemporary Marwari firms in Bengal were Oswals from Jodhpur. These Bengal Oswal families initially settled in Murshidabad (the then capital of Bengal) and its suburbs, Azimganj and Jiaganj. They continued to be particularly prominent in Assam and Bengal and in the jute trade. In Burdwan, the Marwari community was part Oswal and part Aggarwal. By the nineteenth century, the earlier Oswal migrants, now called Murshidabadis, were often large landholders or 'zamindars', having converted their mercantile wealth into land. Particularly in central India, other Marwaris too became zamindars, a fact noted with some alarm by the British at the time because the new merchant-wealth-based landowners were seen as displacing the more 'legitimate', established aristocratic landlords. The large state bankers, the Malpanis in Jabalpur, owned 158 villages. In the late eighteenth and nineteenth centuries, after the establishment of the new British land revenue systems, much of the land changed hands as the old feudal classes often could not manage to pay the taxes;

merchants, including the Marwaris, with newfound wealth decided to invest in land which was seen as a safe asset class. In the nineteenth century, the British were so alarmed by the commercial dominance of the Marwaris and other business communities, and the extent to which they were acquiring land, that laws were passed in several provinces prohibiting 'non-agricultural communities' from acquiring land in rural areas, as also other legislations to curtail the dominance of moneylenders. The British also set up protective regimes like the 'Court of Wards' to protect the indebted zamindars and the larger feudal lords from losing their land.

N.K. Sinha in his 1967 introduction to the reprint of J.H. Little's *The House of Jagatseth* (which originally appeared in the journal *Bengal Past and Present* in 1920-21) blamed Vallal Sen, who ruled Bengal between 1150 and 1179, for the dominance of big non-Bengali merchants in Bengal.[2] In Sen's canonical establishment of caste precedence in Bengal, he placed the Subarnabanik bankers (literally 'gold traders') low because they did not advance him the amount of money that he wanted. Whether this should have been dispositive for all time is for the reader to decide.

The founder of the Jagat Seth house, Hiranand Sahu, came from Nagaur in Marwar to Patna in 1652 and lent money to local rulers as well as to foreign traders there. Manik Chand, his eldest son, moved to Dhaka in the late seventeenth century (the then capital of Bengal and always a key commercial centre) where he was an important commodity trader as well. When Murshid Quli Khan moved the capital of Bengal to Murshidabad (named after him), Manik Chand moved with him. The firm had branches in Hooghly, Calcutta and Varanasi and eventually in Delhi as well. They were, of course, not the only firms there, Marwari or otherwise. In 1789, there were thirteen Armenian, seven Muslim and thirteen 'upcountry Hindu' merchants (like the Jagat Seths) in Dhaka. On his death in 1714, Manik Chand was succeeded by Fateh Chand who was given the title of 'Jagat Seth' by the Mughal emperor in 1722. In 1717, Fateh Chand took charge of the Murshidabad mint, and from that time onwards controlled a great deal of the money economy of Bengal. He financed both local rulers and the major foreign trading companies and was the state treasurer, receiving and allocating public revenues. Between 1718 and 1730, the East India Company took an average credit of Rs 4 lakh per year from the Jagat Seth firm. As late as 1757 they were lending Rs 4 lakh per year to the Dutch East India Company and Rs 15 lakh to the French East India Company.[3]

Though the Jagat Seths supported the British in the politics around the Battle of Plassey in 1757 which firmed British control of Bengal, their position began to decline rapidly as the British took over many of the functions from which the Jagat Seth firm had made money. Their prestige too declined as Calcutta became the commercial centre of Bengal. The firm was not able to successfully enter new areas such as inland trade in which others did well. Further, splits in the family led to long and costly litigations and the firm was partitioned. Even in Murshidabad, by 1791 the largest firm was Manohar Das Dwarka Das, a Varanasi Aggarwal firm which was also a leading banking firm in Surat around the same period. By the nineteenth century the Jagat Seths were forced to request and receive a pension from the British though they continued to be leaders of the Oswal Jain community from which they originated. Sinha concludes his piece with a reference to a discussion with the head of the Jagat Seth family in his reduced state after Independence, presumably in the 1940s or 1950s. He did not have the funds to repair his large palace which was in ruins and had to make do with a smaller one.

3. THE MARWARIS, THE BAZAAR ECONOMY AND THE BRITISH RAJ

AS THE BRITISH established their political control in India especially during the century after the Battle of Plassey, in which they eliminated French competition and secured the control of eastern India, they expanded and reorganized their trading. From being a monopoly affair of the East India Company, the British end of trade itself changed so that it was handled by numerous private trading houses. These trading houses needed partners from the bazaar economy. Initially they dealt with numerous Bengali and other local firms, but as the century progressed Marwari firms spread throughout the hinterlands of Calcutta and to a lesser extent to Bombay and expanded their role as direct intermediaries for the British.

24

Calcutta has several hinterlands: Assam, to where the British advanced in the early nineteenth century and developed tea plantations; East Bengal, from which they eventually drew jute; and the Ganga–Yamuna valley and central India, from which came a variety of goods, especially opium. Through Bombay, the British also traded in cotton and opium. In all areas, the Marwaris traded in imported products like cotton textiles.

Among the prominent firms in Assam, Mahasingh Rai Meghraj Bahadur, which was founded by an Oswal family, descended from the diwans, or prime ministers, of Jaisalmer and Jodhpur. The founder mortgaged his house in Ghertsar in Bikaner to move to Azimganj in 1812. A local Oswal firm then sent him as a clerk to Assam. Mahasingh, the founder of the firm, asked his younger brothers to join him and started his own business. The firm's Calcutta office appears to date from the 1820s. Mahasingh's son, Meghraj (1849–1901), invested in urban real estate and established stores in leading tea plantations and provided banking services as well. At its peak, the firm had eighty-two branches.

The Oswal Jain Dalchand Singhi's family of Azimganj owned Harisingh Nihalchand, a leading jute trading firm in the early twentieth century. Sevairam Singhi came to Azimganj in 1792 and established a firm in Goalpara, then bordering Assam. His son, Raisingh (also known as Harisingh, 1772–1843), was the founder of the main firm. Harisingh's sister was married to the last of the Jagat Seths, Indrachand. The firm eventually acquired several thousand acres of zamindari. Harisingh's great-grandson Dalchand Singhi (1870–1927) was the first president of the Jute Balers' Association. Together with his manager and later partner, Bhairodan Chopra from Gangashahr in Bikaner, Dalchand expanded the firm's activities. In the 1930s, the firm was divided among branches of the family.

Other Oswals and Khandelwal Jains in the jute trade came from Ladnu, Sujangarh, Bidasar and Chapra. Prominent among these were the Bhutorias, originally from Murshidabad. A glance at the ledgers for 1906 of one Bhutoria branch shows a small moneylending business yielding Rs 7500 in interest per year, and trade in cloth, gold and silver, and grain amounting to Rs 3800. Needless to say, with inflation, these would be worth several hundred times that amount today. But these Ladnu Oswals belonged to a different sect of Jains (Digambar and Shvetambar) from the Jagat Seth Oswal group and were clearly separate. The leading Ladnu jute trader Jivanmal Bengani (died 1917), who founded Jivanmal Chandanmal in 1900, was one of the leading jute traders in East Bengal. He was reported to be the first Oswal worth more than one crore rupees and owned a jute mill and markets outside of Calcutta. There were also Oswals from Sardarshahr and Shekhawati who were prominent in Calcutta and in eastern India. Other Oswals were earlier active in Bihar and Orissa.

From the early nineteenth century, Shekhawatis were also prominent in Bihar and Orissa. The Aggarwal Rajgarhias who were major mica dealers moved from Fatehpur Shekhawati to Rajgarh in Bikaner in the middle of the eighteenth century. By 1878, Ganpatrai Rajgarhia (died 1918) had moved to Calcutta. Rajgarhia started dealing in other commodities but an American, at a chance meeting, suggested mica. Rajgarhia quickly established several mines in Bihar. Besides his mica business, his eldest son had a jute mill in 1930. Ganpatrai's younger brother, Juharmal (died 1904), started in the mica business but soon branched out on his own in Raniganj in Bengal, and opened his first mica mine in 1881. By the early 1940s, the Rajgarhias had 8000 employees and offices in London (1912) and elsewhere around the world.

The leading Aggarwal families of Varanasi came from Rajasthan with the Mughals, though this did not prevent some restrictions on intermarriage between them and later Marwari migrants. The old Aggarwals included a number of pioneers of modern Hindi, and their house priests, the Malviyas, included Pandit Madan Mohan

Malviya, the founder of the Banaras Hindu University. However, neither Varanasi nor Lucknow were major Marwari centres before the Second World War. Though there was a significant Marwari presence in Delhi, the Marwaris there were outpaced by businessmen from other business communities. Nonetheless, there were several Marwari-owned textile mills in Delhi. After Independence, however, many Marwari groups started operations in the Delhi area. Later, as the political situation became troubled in Calcutta in the 1960s with the rise of the Communist Party (Marxist), and with the beginning of trade union militancy in Bombay, other Marwari groups shifted their base to a calmer Delhi. In Punjab, too, there was an early and continuing Marwari presence, though indigenous Punjabi business communities were dominant.

In Uttar Pradesh, there was a larger concentration of Shekhawati Marwaris in eastern UP, Hathras, Khurja and Kanpur. A Churu firm, Sadhuram Ramjidas (related to the Great Firm Tarachand Ghanshyamdas which is described at length later in this book) dominated the Kanpur market until the firm's partition in 1840. This firm had earlier been partners with the Jatia family, which produced one of the leading Marwari *banians* (partners to foreign firms), Sir Onkar Mal Jatia.

In Kanpur, one of the most important early firms

was Sevaram Ramrikhdas, which belonged to the Singhanjas (from which the modern J.K. group and its various descendants emerged). A city history of Kanpur lists twenty-seven Marwari firms, forty Punjabi firms and ten–fifteen others. Several firms, including that of Sevaram Ramrikhdas, arrived soon after the War of Independence in 1857 from Farrukhabad. Other prominent eastern UP Marwaris include the Khetans from Alsisar in Shekhawati, who started business in Padrauna. They opened a branch in Calcutta in 1893, one in Bombay in 1917 and another in Kanpur in 1921. They eventually had three sugar mills, a share in a jute mill and a textile mill as well as 9000 acres of sugar cane land. The role of the family of Motilal Jhunjhunwala, the silver king, in the UP sugar industry is detailed later in this book. There were other Marwari firms prominent in the grain and cloth trade.

The migration of Marwari traders was furthered by the branch network of the Great Firms, which is explained in detail later. These firms already had branches in Calcutta in the first half of the nineteenth century, but it is in the second half of the century that Marwaris, especially the Shekhawati Marwaris, became the primary banians for foreign firms, controlling their supply chains, and played a key role in the development of the stock, commodity and other speculative markets. It was these roles which enabled them to become industrial entrepreneurs especially after the First World War and more so after Independence.

Other Shekhawati Marwaris were involved in the development of the Jharia coalfields in Bengal. Firms connected with Fulchand Goenka, from Churu in Shekhawati, had two coal mines, one from 1910 and another which they took on lease in 1925.

The 1945 Gazetteer for Darjeeling district reports:

> The Marwari dominates most of the exporting trades viz. cardamom, oranges and potatoes and practically all the import trade of consumption goods. In addition, he has an almost complete control of the retail sale of consumption goods to, and of the purchase of produce from the small consumer and producer.

The Shekhawati Marwaris were already a major presence in central India in the eighteenth century, and by 1820 had a presence throughout the Indo-Gangetic Plain. This presence continued and grew throughout the nineteenth and twentieth centuries. However, it was only after 1820 that they appeared in large numbers in Calcutta and Bombay.

Though the Marwari role in Bombay and Madras was less pronounced than in Calcutta, it was not negligible. But it was the indigenous south Indian and Gujarati business communities which controlled those markets that the Marwaris dominated in the east. Marwari firms in Bombay were major suppliers of cotton and opium by the middle of the nineteenth century but were less prominent than the Gujarati groups.

The Bazaar Economy Copes with the Boxwallahs

There were three major approaches by way of which Marwari businessmen related to the new British-dominated economy—these included the emergence of three types of enterprises. First, the Great Firms, the large state bankers and long-distance traders who had all along been active in long-distance trade, and who continued to play that role. Second, formal banians or guaranteed brokers to the large foreign firms. Third, firms which participated in and finally dominated the dynamic wholesale and higher level futures and ready markets for shares and commodities, as traders and speculators.

Great Firms

The 'Great Firms' were large firms, often some centuries old. Some Somani and Poddar firms of today trace their main firms to the eighteenth century. These Great Firms were comparable in many respects to the European (many of them of Jewish origin) firms of families such as the Rothschilds, Mendelssohns, Philipsons, Bleichroeders, Warburgs, Koenigswaters, etc., which had served rulers in northern Europe and expanded, after the Napoleonic Wars, to form the framework for international trade and finance. The main Warburg firm and N.M. Rothschild were both founded in 1798, based on older family firms.

The Indian Great Firms had a network of branches and affiliates all over India and sometimes in other parts of the world, within which they ferried commodities and transferred funds. Because of this they were able to offer banking facilities to other firms (for transferring and borrowing money), insurance (originally connected with the armed convoys they often organized), and probably most importantly, business intelligence. They explicitly provided the capital, management skill and business intelligence which otherwise was not available at that time.

The Great Firms formed part of a more general business support system. Allan R. Cohen describes the mutual credit system used by Marwari traders in Varanasi:

Firms in the system borrowed from each other whenever short of cash, loans were payable on demand, 'even at midnight,' and interest was tallied and settled once a year, with total borrowing offset by total lending.[1]

To continue from my 1978 book:[2]

Community banks provided accommodation for goods in transit and remittance facilities. Communal customs provided for apprenticeships in which youngsters could learn the techniques of business, and profit-sharing schemes by which they could accumulate enough capital to start their own enterprises.[3] Communal or sometimes inter-communal institutions existed for adjudicating disputes.[4]

Records recount two charitable messes for Marwaris working in Calcutta, in the early twentieth century, run by Nathuram Saraf of Mandawa and Surajmal Jhunjhunwala of Chirawa, two towns in the Shekhawati region from which many successful businessmen came. G.D. Birla's grandfather, Shiv Narain, settled in a *basa* run on a cooperative basis by migrants from his home village of Pilani when he first arrived in Bombay in the 1860s. Besides providing food and a place to sleep, the messes were informal training schools and networking opportunities for newly arrived Marwari businessmen. One commentator says that a leading businessman compared them favourably with Harvard Business School. Perhaps they sometimes even used the 'case method' in their mess discussions.

The Great Firms had elaborate systems for obtaining, transmitting and using business intelligence. It is interesting that historians of both the Rothschilds and the Birlas report various systems for relaying business news—carrier pigeons, signal mirrors and other means of transmitting news quickly—before the advent of the telegraph. The stories might be apocryphal but it is reported that the first British Rothschilds made their fortune when their communications system told them of the victory at Waterloo ahead of others and they were able to use the knowledge to score on the London Stock Exchange. One of the earliest uses of the English language by Indian businessmen was to read telegrams, which could only be transmitted in English, as several report in their biographies. This element of special techniques for commercial intelligence keeps recurring in the histories of successes in the speculative markets. Motilal Jhunjhunwala, the silver king of the pre–Second World War period, was reported to have a radio system, albeit illegal, in operation.

But the telegraph also provides the model for the assimilation of modern technology. It foreshadows the mechanization and routinization of previously arcane business processes such as bookkeeping, and financial management in general.

The market itself was organized with various sorts of

informal and formal panchayats and market committees which arbitrated and mediated commercial disputes, enacted various rules, maintained common facilities and represented the merchant community to the outside world, especially to the British authorities. As explained later in the book, mediation by larger businessmen continues in family-firm partition disputes, as exemplified by Jai Dayal Dalmia in the Motilal Jhunjhunwala case, and in various takeover bids.

*

The Marwari Great Firms were frequently state financiers and often began business as treasurers to one or more ruler. Historically, such firms combined state financing with trade, finance (which included insurance and remittance services) and even infrastructure investment. In Europe, the services of the financier to the feudal lord often extended to managing the owner's mill, distillery and even inn. As the quote attributed to the Medicis has it, these business families used wealth to get power and power to get wealth.

The Great Firms were companies with multiple activities, a large branch network involved in trade, state finance, banking (which included lending, borrowing and remitting money, insurance) and occasionally manufacture. Typically, family firms were prototypes of the modern 'business group'. A number of the leading Great Firms by the eighteenth and nineteenth centuries originated from Rajasthan. Some of these were from Shekhawati, like Tarachand Ghanshyamdas. Bikaneri Marwaris also owned several important Great Firms, such as Bansilal Abirchand which became the key British banking firm in central India; several Bikaneri Marwari families became prominent as bankers to the Nizams of Hyderabad. Chief among these were the Pittys who arrived in Hyderabad in 1817, apparently from Jahazpur in Bhilwara. Another family firm conspicuous in banking belonged to the Daddas from Phalodi in Jodhpur State.

Tarachand Ghanshyamdas: A Model Great Firm

Tarachand Ghanshyamdas was one of the most famous Great Firms. The Calcutta *Bengal Hurkaru* newspaper (an early-nineteenth-century edited English newspaper) in 1834 reported:

> The only people who carry on regular trade in European commodities, with the countries beyond the Indus and the Sutlej, are the Banians of Jodhpur and Shekhavati countries, who are known by the general name of Marwaris . . . they may be said to be the only merchants in Upper India.

The following instance will help to illustrate the extended scale of Marwari connections:

Mirzamal, Fakirchand, Johurimal and Haikunt Rai are the grandsons of a person called Bhagoti Ram, who was the Podar or treasurer to then Nawab of Fatehpur in the Shekhavati country, as well as at Churu in the Bikaner country, which is only 5 kos [10 miles] off, and they live at either one place or the other . . .

Someone or other of the twelve Poddars have Gomasthas or Agents in the following places . . . that is—Bombay, Surat, Muscat, Pali, Jodhpur, Nagore, Jugadri, Hissar, Indore, Nagpur, Hyderabad, Poona, Hathras, Chandausi, Farrukhabad, Mathura, Agra, Mirzapur, Benares, Murshidibad, Patna, Calcutta, Goalpura. These Gomashtas are all of them from Churu, from Bikaner and Ramgarh, Bisau, Fatehpur, and Jhunjhunu in the Shekhavati country. They are everywhere distinguished as foreigners by their language and dress, and their families reside in their own country.[5]

Bhagoti Ram Poddar founded the firm which was the ancestor to Tarachand Ghanshyamdas in the early eighteenth century. He had been a banker to the Nawab of Fatehpur and also served the rulers of Bikaner and the Punjab. Following the defeat of the Nawab by Rao Raja of Sikar in 1731, the firm of Tarachand Ghanshyamdas was set up in its latter-day form. Other sources connect the foundation of the firm with the Pindari Nawabs, whom the Poddars also served as bankers.

Bhagoti Ram had been living in Churu. A Jain monk told him to go to Bhatinda in the Punjab to trade in wool and it was there that he made his fortune. While trade with the British in the nineteenth century constituted a new key industry, wool trade out of Kashmir was an ancient arena of business. Bhagoti's son, Chaterbhuj, set up branches dealing in wool trade in Amritsar, Bhatinda and Hissar. He also led a merchants' resistance movement against a wool tax imposed by the thakur of Churu.

As was the case with many such anti-tax movements in feudal India, this one led to the migration of the Poddars to Ramgarh in the neighbouring jurisdiction of Sikar, a premodern equivalent of the tax havens of Switzerland or Singapore. In Ramgarh, the Poddars and their allies built their own city state. Foreign travellers marvelled at the town's prosperity and security.

Among the prominent Poddar firms which descended from Bhagoti Ram were Sojiram Hardayal, Anantram Shivprasad, Harsamal Ramchandra, Sevaram Kaluram and Johurimal Ramlal, all of which had branches in Calcutta. The main firm was continued by Chaterbhuj's son, Tarachand. Tarachand Ghanshyamdas was in the opium trade in Malwa through Bombay and dealt in gold and wool, banking and insurance. Tarachand died at an early age leaving two sons, Gursahaymal and Harsahaymal, known as 'Gursa Harsa' as a unit. The firm was divided between them in 1823–24. Harsahaymal's descendants did business as Harsahaymal Ramchandra.

Chaterbhuj had three sons: Johurimal, Jindaram and Tarachand. Johurimal founded the firm Johurimal Ramlal. Jindaram lived in Churu. A published extract from a ledger reveals the conclusion of an opium purchase for Rs 311 in Churu in 1787. Jindaram's son, Mirzamal, was associated with Ranjit Singh, the last powerful ruler of the Punjab, from the time he was starting out as a local chieftain.

Gursahaymal died in 1868 leaving a son, Tarachand Ghanshyamdas, who died in 1885 leaving five sons. The two eldest sons, Jainarain and Lakshminarain, separated from the main firm in 1868. Ghanshyamdas's younger sons, Radhakrishen and Keshavdas, became the heads of the firm Tarachand Ghanshyamdas, while their youngest brother, Murlidhar, became an ascetic.

Despite Tarachand Ghanshyamdas's commercial operations being in Calcutta, the owners continued to reside in Ramgarh and later moved to various pilgrimage centres in northern India. The active management of the firm was in the hands of its chief managers, especially Harduttrai Prahladhka and Jainarain Poddar.

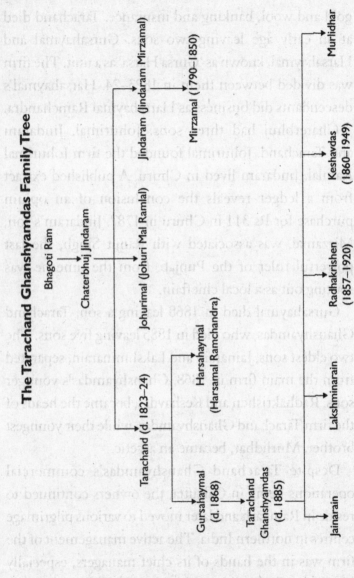

The Tarachand Ghanshyamdas Family Tree

Bhagoti Ram → Chaterbhuj Jindaram → Jindaram (Jindaram Mirzamal)

Mirzamal (1790–1850) → Murlidhar, Keshavdas (1860–1949), Radhakrishen (1857–1920)

Johurimal (Johuri Mal Ramlal) → Tarachand (d. 1823–24)

Harsahaymal (Harsamal Ramchandra)

Gursahaymal (d. 1868) → Tarachand Ghanshyamdas (d. 1885)

Lakshminarain, Jainarain

The opium business was in rapid decline and abolished in the early twentieth century. In 1896, the firm started a selling agency for Asiatic Petroleum Company and its successors, the Burmah Oil Company and Shaw Wallace (a major British trading conglomerate and managing agency).[6] This entailed setting up a network of 800 branches throughout India, many of which also engaged in other businesses. For example, the Karachi branch was a major commission-procuring agent for agricultural produce from the Punjab. The firm thus began to transform itself into the next category of firm, the banian or broker to foreign firms.

Tarachand Ghanshyamdas: The Structure of the Great Firm

The operations of Tarachand Ghanshyamdas around 1914 were typical. Everywhere the branches of the firm were located in rented premises with rooms decked with gaddis, white cotton cloth–covered mattresses stuffed with cotton or straw and strewn with business paraphernalia like traditional red cloth–covered ledgers and cash boxes. 'Gaddi' referred both to the mattresses and the rooms in which they were located, and could be comparable to a king's throne. The branch was supervised by a chief manager or munim with several sub-managers or *gomashta*s. In the rear of the office there were warehouses or godowns for the storage of goods (the stock in trade). Also somewhere in the rear were the kitchens for the mess or basa. The gaddi was also used for sleeping. Keeping guard of the gaddi were watchmen or 'durwans'. They were doormen but with somewhat different functions than those in a Manhattan apartment in New York. This was a tradition common to many firms in Calcutta. The durwans were Chaturvedi Brahmins or 'Chaubes' from the Mathura region and were traditionally wrestlers. Later, some went into the stock exchange and did quite well. But in general, the Chaturvedis were an elite 'service' caste. In a sense, the Chaturvedis were like the Nepali Gurkha guards of today, a common sight in the posher areas of Indian cities.

Each gomashta had a separate kind of ledger. There was a *khatavahi* containing separate accounts for each class of business; a *hundi-nukl* in which copies of all Hundis or indigenous bills of trade were entered and a *jama-vahi* holding a record of the physical goods' inventory. There was a cash book or *rokarvahi* in which all cash transactions were entered and could be checked against other records, and a ledger, the final balance of the firm's accounts. Telegrams zipped back and forth between branches to update these. Daily reports of the cash-and-credit position had to be sent to the main office.

There was a traditional Gujarati banking firm in the 1980s where the brothers (partners as well) did a series of long-distance calls at the end of each day to update their cash position. The Reserve Bank of India did away with these traditional Gujarati bankers by a regulation it issued in the 1980s.

Until the First World War, the Tarachand Ghanshyamdas office or gaddi at 18, Mullick Street in Calcutta took up an entire floor of Kaligodam, a large multistorey building near the old centre of the opium trade, built in the 1870s. The firm took up more than eight rooms, opening on to a balcony overlooking a central courtyard. There were eight–nine clerks working there. The head manager, Chhaganlal Bhavsinghka, was paid the princely sum of Rs 250 a month and owned his own grain mill over the main gate of the building. The regular clerks were paid between Rs 50–60 a month. There were several durwans. Five are recorded in 1872–73. None were paid more than Rs 200 a year. There were several Brahmin cooks for the basa. The salaries were generous for the era and remarked on as such by those who remembered the period in the early 1970s.

Managers and clerks in 1914 were mostly Shekhawati Aggarwals like the Poddars themselves. The names that are recorded were from Ramgarh, Mukundgarh and Churu but we are told that 90 per cent of Tarachand

Ghanshyamdas's clerks were Aggarwals and about 10 per cent were Brahmins.

Besides their pay, the managers often received a share in the profits of the firm. Jainarain Poddar, the chief manager, testified in court that he received Rs 2–3 lakh annually over a period of several years, probably his share of the profits. Other branch managers had variously defined shares in profits. The exact arrangements differed from firm to firm. Two other Great Firms, Bansilal Abirchand of Nagpur and Mahasingh Rai Meghraj Bahadur, the latter concentrated in Assam, did not offer a share in profits to their managers. Some other Great Firms preferred Brahmin clerks to those from their own caste because it was perceived that they would be less likely to enter into competition with the original firm and considered less aggressive.

The managers were regularly rotated and promoted. Harduttrai Prahladhka joined the firm in 1860 in Calcutta, and moved to the Mathura and Ramgarh branches, before leaving the firm. He returned as a branch manager to Calcutta in 1896. Jainarain Poddar had been in the banking business with his father in Hyderabad from 1865 to 1873 and joined the firm in 1883–84. He seems to have worked for some time in branches concentrating on opium in Malwa. He later moved to Kanpur and finally to Calcutta in 1896. He succeeded Harduttrai Prahladhka as branch manager in 1912. In 1920, he received a share in the profits of the firm, and in 1930, this was increased to a five-sixteenth share.

Bansilal Abirchand, another Great Firm, had its headquarters in Bikaner where its owners, the Dagas, had been located since 1598. However, its operations were centred in Nagpur and Indore. The firm assisted the British during the War of 1857 and was suitably rewarded. The offshoots of the Great Firms that prospered in the nineteenth century were often those that were the closest to the British in India. As a consequence, they reaped the considerable rewards that the British gave to those who could be counted among the loyal in 1857. By 1908, Bansilal Abirchand owned forty-seven villages, two cotton mills, twenty gins and presses, and a multiple-branch banking business. British officers in smaller towns often kept their accounts with the firm. During the post–First World War period, it would transfer Rs 3 crore every year to cover its seasonal trading operations in Burma. But the branch managers, as early as the 1880s, only submitted semi-annual returns to the home office. Each branch of Bansilal Abirchand would function as an independent unit. For example, though the firm's four branches in Nagpur concentrated on banking, gold, grain and cloth, they dealt in whatever was opportune. The branch managers held wide-ranging powers of attorney to act on behalf of the firm. However, this degree of decentralization was exceptional. In contrast, Goculdas Malpani of Jabalpur spent nine months of the year on the road checking the books of accounts at his branches.

The Malpanis of the firm Sevaram Khushalchand were Maheshwaris from Jaisalmer. Sevaram Malpani moved to Jabalpur in central India in the early nineteenth century. He started a series of branch offices and entered the banking business. Sevaram Khushalchand also served as a leading banking firm to the British and was rewarded for its assistance and loyalty during the 1857 War of Independence. A British official reports a transaction apparently in the early twentieth century:

> It would be untactful to start straightaway on business as the chief motive of the visit, though the motive is tacitly understood. So we exchange the usual elaborate greetings in the hyperbole of Hindustani—for the great man knows no English. Then general topics, such as the weather, crop prospects, the probability of epidemic disease in the city, and I make inquiry about the Raja's stables, a favourite subject . . . Meanwhile the fountain plays . . . and time slips away. Then at last the question comes—is there any service which the Sahib wishes done? I reply that there is a trifling matter, a little money to be remitted. The great man beckons an attendant, who removes the

sack without counting coin or notes. That doesn't matter; I know it will be all right. More compliments and talk. The attendant reappears with the sack, now empty. We ignore him and continue the leisurely talk, till the Raja asks in feigned surprise, as though he had forgotten all about it, whether we hadn't some small business to do. Ah yes; here it is. He takes a tiny scrap of paper from the attendant and hands it to me. All it contains are a few hieroglyphics in the obscure Marwari script. This I pocket with ostentatious negligence, well knowing that in a few days I shall receive an acknowledgement from the British bank in the capital of a neighbouring province.[7]

The Malpanis also purchased several hundred villages in which they served as zamindars though, unlike some of the businessmen in Bengal, they did not give up their trading and banking. Their twentieth-century heir, Seth Gobind Das Malpani (1896–1974), was a Congress activist and Hindi literateur who served as a member of parliament—I met him in the 1960s, and our discussion revealed the extensive nature of his English education.

*

The Great Firms business groups operated in a context of business communities which embodied certain cultural traits and values which were functional to business and business continuity. These are values that are still manifest in traditional firms in the modern period. Some of these are well documented in a number of business biographies and autobiographies connected with the Birla family. The founder of the Birla family business group, Shiv Narain, had connections with Tarachand Ghanshyamdas as well as with the great Ganeriwala firm. He finally started his own firm which he passed on to his son, Raja Baldevdas, and his four grandsons Jugal Kishore, Rameshwar Das, Ghanshyamdas and Brij Mohan, and their descendants. Though they emerged from working with the Great Firms, the Birlas were more prominent first as business partners to British and other foreign firms, then as speculators on the Indian markets, and finally as industrialists following a trajectory which has been seen to characterize many of the leading Marwari family business groups of today.

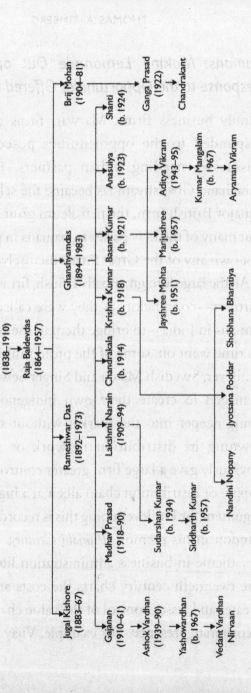

The Birla Family Tree

*Banians: Making Lemonade Out of Lemons—
Response to the Opportunities Offered by the British*

Family business firms, Marwari firms among them,
responded to the opportunities posed by foreign
businesses needing Indian partners. For example,
Tarachand Ghanshyamdas became the selling agent for
a major British firm, the petroleum giant, Burmah Oil.
But many of the new partners, banians in particular, did
not own any of the Great Firms themselves.

All the large foreign, mostly British, firms, needed local
partners—compradors as they were called in China or
banians in India—to bridge them to the Indian market.
As time went on, some of the proto multinationals like
Unilever, Swedish Match and Singer Sewing Machines
managed to create their own indigenous networks,
going deeper into the market without such partners.
Owning its distribution network or supply chain
obviously gave a large firm greater control over its own
supply or distribution chain albeit at a higher cost. The
argument for Unilever doing this is recorded by Prakash
Tandon in his memoir, *Punjabi Century, 1857-1947*. A
key theme in business administration literature in the
late twentieth century charts the costs and benefits of
greater and lesser control of the value chain in building
a corporate presence. For example, Vijay Govindarajan

and Gunjan Bagla penned an article in the 19 October 2012 *Harvard Business Review*, 'Watch Out for India's Consumer Market Pitfalls', arguing against relying on a single distributor for all of India, partly because of the regionally differentiated nature of Indian consumer markets. Gurcharan Das in *India Unbound* discusses at some length his discovery of the value of locally based stockists who know the local market as he worked to develop Vicks VapoRub's market in India.[8]

But new entrants still needed partners. Even today one of the standard pieces of advice to a new market entrant in India or elsewhere is the value of a local partner for navigating that market. In fact, even multinationals need lower level stockists and suppliers. Then, as it is now, a strong local partner was often a critical element in success.

Originally, banians had a broader function of intermediation but they were eventually reduced to 'guaranteed brokers', so called because they guaranteed the commercial soundness of various underbrokers. The banian's approval was necessary for sales and they allocated the stock among dealers. Sir Badridas Goenka mentioned that underbrokers would visit his brother Sir Hari Ram Goenka in his suburban garden home on Saturdays to secure their allocation of imported cloth. Sir Hari Ram was the 'sole broker' to Ralli Brothers, a large commodity trader and cloth importer. The guaranteed broker was usually given a 1 per cent commission. Underbrokers only received 0.25 per cent commission on cotton piece goods. The guaranteed brokers were also expected to provide a large deposit which was, of course, a useful part of the foreign firm's capital.

The banians to British firms in Calcutta were originally Bengalis. An exhaustive list in 1863 shows only one non-Bengali firm. Later members of the Khatri caste from the Punjab displaced some of the Bengalis, adding this to the prominent role they had always played in the wool trade out of the Punjab in which the Marwaris too were actively engaged. In an interview with me in 1971, one of the heirs of a great Khatri firm attributed their decline to high overheads and the lack of a sufficiently extensive upcountry network. The Khatris were soon replaced by the Marwaris. Banians in Madras were usually from various local trading communities or Brahmins, and those in Bombay were usually Parsees or Gujarati Bhatias.

In contrast to older industries like imported cotton piece goods in which indigenous firms played a dominant role, the presence of banians in the east Indian jute trade was lower because European firms were already better established. In the hessian and woven-fabric space of the jute industry, Indian firms had to fight for a place which was accorded to them only reluctantly. The jute mills and exporters dealt directly with European agents as late as the First World War. The Birlas report that they had to retain a European broker; a Calcutta Jewish broker, who counted as European for this purpose, was among their earliest business associates. Maria Misra in her seminal book, *Business, Race, and Politics in British India, c.1850–1960*, attributes the decline of the old British business houses, in contrast to the newer multinationals, to their reluctance to enter into full partnership with Indian firms.[9] Dwijendra Tripathi suggests that the British groups' decline responded to the general weakness of the Indian economy in the 1920s and 1930s. This exclusion of Indian firms was not possible in raw-jute trade, where the Marwari firms with their network across rural Bengal were critical.

For raw jute, it appeared that only the Marwaris had an adequate upcountry trading network, including areas like Assam and Bengal which fed into Calcutta. In raw jute, the European sellers got a 1.25 per cent commission of which they passed 0.25 per cent to their Indian brokers. The 1915 Hisar Gazetteer notes that migrants from Bhiwani (an area adjoining Rajasthan) were already important hessian and fabric traders. The pioneers in hessian and fabric trade included entrepreneurs from areas other than Bhiwani as well such as Lakshmi Narain Kanoria, closely connected with McLeod and Company from 1887, M.D. Somani and G.D. Birla. The latter two were well known as hessian traders since 1915.

By the First World War, the Calcutta market was dominated by a number of 'big banians' who did business as banians in the nineteenth century. Some of the Great Firms also became banians, like Tarachand Ghanshyamdas for Shaw Wallace and Burmah Oil. Devkarandas Ramkumar Chokhani of Nawalgarh was listed as a banian to Ludwig Duke in 1878. Gursahaymal Ghanshyamdas (related to Tarachand Ghanshyamdas) was already a banian to Crook and Rowe prior to 1860, and Sevaram Ramrikhdas, the firm originally based in Mirzapur from which sprang the Singhania family of Kanpur (one of the largest of contemporary business groups), was a banian to Ralli Brothers. But soon a number of others emerged—not descended—from the owners of the Great Firms. Ramdutt Goenka was the chief Calcutta clerk for Sevaram Ramrikhdas. Besides his own Goenka firm, the heirs of which are still prominent in Calcutta business, including the RPG Group, he gave initial support to Nathuram Saraf, who was by tradition the first Marwari banian. The newer banian firms and the old firms were closely linked by commercial and marital ties.

The reputed first Marwari banian, Nathuram Saraf, came to Calcutta in the 1830s as a supercargo in one of Sevaram Ramrikhdas's boats from Mirzapur. He became a banian to Kinsell and Ghose. This was a Bengali–European partnership of a sort, once common but which declined after the 1848 financial panic, and which sunk the fortunes of Dwarkanath Tagore (Rabindranath Tagore's grandfather) whose firm, Carr Tagore, was the largest of them. According to historical accounts, Nathuram displaced Nikkamal Khatri, then a leading banian, to become a banian to Hoare Miller. Nathuram called upon a large number of fellow villagers from Mandawa in Shekhawati to enter business in Calcutta and set up separate basas for the Brahmins and Banias. In 1870, he retired to Rajasthan where he worked as a banker to a number of princes. His business passed on to his head clerk, Ganeshdas Musuddi (died 1882), whose family continued to work as banians well into the 1930s.

Most banians did not retire to become bankers but continued as banians for several generations. The Goenka family, descendants of Ramdutt, produced many banians. Initially Ramdutt was associated with Sevaram Ramrikhdas as a banian to Kinsell and Ghose but after 1848, he became a broker to Kettlewell Bullen, founding his own firm, Ramdutt Ramkissendas. He also became a banian to Ralli Brothers, the largest cloth importer, as well as being an important participant in other markets. Apparently, Sevaram Ramrikhdas had been the banian to Ralli Brothers earlier. Shivbaksh, Ramdutt's nephew, was working with Rallis as early as 1864. When Shivbaksh resigned in 1880 because of certain differences with the Rallis management, Ramchandra, a grandson of Ramdutt, was made banian, though the Goenkas continued their relationship with Kettlewell Bullen as well. Ramchandra was succeeded as banian by his sons, Sir Hari Ram (1862–1932), Ghanshyamdas (born 1868) and Sir Badridas (1883–1973).

Similar to the Goenkas' association with Rallis was Surajmal Jhunjhunwala's relationship with Graham & Co. Lalchand Kayah (died 1875) came to Calcutta in the 1830s from Surajgarh. He established a firm, Lalchand Baldevdas, trading in commodities like opium and cotton throughout eastern India. Lalchand's son-in-law Surajmal Jhunjhunwala (1850–1894) arrived in Calcutta in 1867, and by January 1868 had become a metal broker to the large Bengali-owned firm, Pran Kissen Law. He soon moved to cotton piece goods and then transferred his activities to Smellie & Co. In April 1868, he was back with Pran Kissen Law as senior broker and soon also became a broker to another Law family firm headed by Abhay Charan Law. In March 1879, Pran Kissen Law became sole piece goods broker to Graham & Co. Later, the banianship was taken over by Surajmal. At this time, Surajmal was also managing the Musuddi banianship at Hoare Miller and at Gladstone Wright as the heirs to the

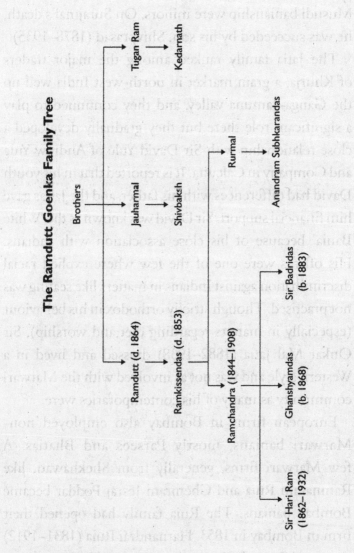

The Ramdutt Goenka Family Tree

Brothers

— Tugan Ram — Kedarnath

— Jauharmal — Shivbaksh

— Ramdutt (d. 1864) — Ramkissendas (d. 1853) — Rurmal — Anandram Subhkarandas
— Ramchandra (1844–1908)
  — Sir Badridas (b. 1883)
  — Ghanshyamdas (b. 1868)
  — Sir Hari Ram (1862–1932)

Musudi banianship were minors. On Surajmal's death, he was succeeded by his son, Shivprasad (1878–1935).

The Jatia family ranked among the major traders of Khurja, a grain market in north-west India well up the Ganga–Jamuna valley, and they continued to play a significant role there but they gradually developed a close relationship with Sir David Yule of Andrew Yule and Company in Calcutta. It is reported that in his youth David had differences with his father, and the Jatias gave him financial support. Sir David was known as the 'White Bania' because of his close association with Indians. His offices were one of the few where explicit racial discrimination against Indians in matters like seating was not practised. Though strictly orthodox in his behaviour (especially in matters regarding diet and worship), Sir Onkar Mal Jatia (1882–1938) dressed and lived in a Western style and was not as involved with the Marwari community as many of his contemporaries were.

European firms in Bombay also employed non-Marwari banians, mostly Parsees and Bhatias. A few Marwari firms, generally from Shekhawati, like Ramnarain Ruia and Cheniram Jesraj Poddar became Bombay banians. The Ruia family had opened their firm in Bombay in 1853. Harnandrai Ruia (1831–1912) separated from the business and specialized in opium. One of his four sons, Ramnarain, became a broker to the opium department of Sassoon J. David (not to be confused with David Sassoon or E.D. Sassoon and Company, though he married into the original David Sassoon's family),[10] one of Bombay's leading Jewish firms in 1883. In 1891, Ramnarain became a guaranteed broker to that firm's cotton department. The Ruias soon became major players in the cotton market though they did not start a mill of their own until 1934.

Anandilal Poddar, one of the more prominent Bombay Marwari businessmen, was born in 1874 in Nawalgarh. He first went to Calcutta in 1891 and then to Dibrugarh in Assam but finally settled in Bombay in 1895. Though Anandilal started as a clerk in another firm he soon set up his own brokerage firm, dealing particularly with Japanese firms. In 1919, he became chief broker to Toyo Menka Kaisha (Mitsui), and in 1926 set up a cotton textile mill in association with them

The Marwari firm, Cheniram Jesraj from Bisau, not far from Ramgarh, was founded in Bombay prior to 1880. The founder, who died in 1887, had been an opium broker to the Parsee Tatas. The firm provided the sole selling agency for four Tata textile mills.

Following a stereotype, the banian firms were more socially and culturally conservative than non-banian firms, both in terms of overall cultural attitudes and in terms of new economic activities. Though they were not the first to start new industries, a number of them did emerge as major industrial firms when they acquired the British interests with which they had been associated, after Indian independence. Among the leading Marwari groups of today, many have descended from major banian firms. Consequently, many of the old banian families today have in their possession companies they acquired from the British. Of the large business groups of today, the Singhanias emerged from a Great Firm, the Birlas were pre-eminent in trading in commodity markets and the RPG Group is descended from Ramdutt Ramkissendas, a leading banian.

Speculation: The Art of Managing Risk

Finally, a considerable number of the larger Marwari business groups made their money in the speculative markets of the nineteenth century and especially in the early twentieth century during the First and Second World Wars. These funds they then sometimes invested in new industrial ventures.

Though records of the great speculators are under-documented, there exists a body of anecdotes and stories which emphasizes how much they operated on intuition, perhaps based on superior commercial intelligence, and maybe even inside information before tapping into such information became illegal. Niall Ferguson emphasizes the same characteristics in the operation of the early Rothschild firm which is particularly well documented in the thousands of letters between the partners; these have been preserved and have only recently become generally available.[11]

We can also trace the evanescence of speculators. Keshoram Poddar lost all his wealth, and continued à la Warren Buffett to live right through in the same modest apartment. Motilal Jhunjhunwala did not have heirs who were successful speculators. Many of the firms that speculators left behind ended up riven with litigation and family infighting.

All business involves some risk. The management of that risk is a key management task. Businessmen, especially entrepreneurs and those who launch new enterprises, are risk-takers. As a consequence, some businessmen seek risk or try to make a business out of handling it and in the process become professional speculators or, euphemistically, 'risk managers'.

Some of the risk is simply borne, for a price. Some is insured against. But some is bought and sold on speculative markets. It is on these markets that a 'killing' can be made. George Soros became a billionaire from betting against the British pound. Like horse racing, the betting does not occur in a vacuum but in a world in which information about the factors likely to influence prices is considered.

Most of the speculation is constrained both by the narrow limits within which prices are expected to move and the limited financial capacity of speculators. Many participants in speculative markets hedge, which means that they take a position that reduces their risks and uncertainties as well as their potential profits. Thus, a flour mill company may buy options to purchase wheat, a key input, in the future at certain prices to reduce its risk of fluctuations. Those companies with future obligations in dollars may buy options to purchase dollars at specific prices when they will need to pay them out. Sometimes, the hedgers will both buy an option to purchase and to sell to constrain the range of their risk. But other speculation is done for its own sake, as a business activity.

A part of the impulse that leads to speculation is undoubtedly a desire to gamble, and speculators often gamble on sports events. But economic speculation is also pursued as a strategy for risk management for normal business or as a separate business by businessmen who specialize in it.

Speculative markets have existed for as long as trading has, and the spreading Marwari diaspora was involved in these markets from an early point in their history—the Victorian British rulers of India and their modern Indian successors were not always pleased by this. A whole body of literature exists on the conflicts that this entailed and has been documented by anthropologists.[12] The press was full of records of British–Indian police raids on speculative markets and this continued in independent India too. As one government source in the British period said, 'A large amount of the professionally owned capital of the district is diverted from the legitimate operations of trade to speculation, or more correctly to gambling by means of anticipation bargains, "vaida".'[13] Raids on speculative markets were sporadic.[14]

The issue remains alive. The post-Independence Indian government suppressed a broad variety of speculative markets and it is only relatively recently that they have been permitted, and even then slowly and with some hesitation. Even though the hedging function is recognized, there is anxiety that in India these markets will be subject to manipulation and somehow act against the interests of 'productive businessmen'.

More generally, the rise of interest in Islamic or sharia finance has focused attention on the differences between real (inevitable and permitted) and artificial (independently generated and forbidden) risk.

S.M. Edwardes in his classic *Gazetteer of Bombay* notes:

The Mercantile and Moneyed classes in the city perform

an enormous amount of speculative business on behalf of upcountry constituents . . . in Government Promissory notes . . . the shares of joint companies, in cotton, in oil seeds . . . in wheat, in Rangoon rice, in Calcutta-made gunny bags, and in gold and silver.[15]

A British visitor in the 1870s noted that the home areas of Shekhawati and Bikaner already had vigorous speculative markets. Regular speculation on opium in Bombay and Calcutta seemed to have started on an organized basis in the 1830s.

I have seen entries in Marwari ledgers, as early as 1791, entering speculative transactions, *fatka*, which refers almost certainly to the so-called rain bargains. These were bets on the date when the monsoons would arrive. On the one hand, in the broader sense, when the rainy season will start is the most obvious thing to speculate on in the hot north Indian summer; on the other hand, it is a datum of crucial economic significance given its impact on the harvest. As Basil Blackett, not John Maynard Keynes as some report, notoriously said, the Indian economy then, and even to some extent now, is a wager on the monsoons.[16]

Personalities such as Harduttrai Chamaria (1872–1916) and Sir Swarupchand Hukumchand (1874–1959) were the 'kings' of speculative markets. Harduttrai

Chamaria's family came to Calcutta from Fatehpur in Shekhawati in the 1840s. The family became brokers to the wealthy Bombay-based Ismaili Currimbhoy Ebrahim family (later made baronets by the British). Harduttrai partitioned the family firm with his brother Ram Pratap in 1903 and the partition deed included a fair amount of Calcutta real estate. As early as 1900 we find Harduttrai invited to the Viceroy's levees and given the title of 'Seth' by the Maharaja of Jaipur.

Hukumchand's family owned the largest banking firm dealing with Indore state. During 1909–10, when the British started restricting the number of opium boxes for export, the Indian market weakened. Hukumchand bought Rs 20–25 lakh worth of opium on credit. The price skyrocketed ten times, and Hukumchand mopped up Rs 2 crore. In 1911, Harduttrai was the key organizer in a syndicate including, among others, Jugal Kishore Birla, G.D. Birla's elder brother, which made a killing on the opium market. Sir Hukumchand made Rs 1 crore in 1914–15 and Rs 75 lakh in 1918–19 based on successful cotton market corners.

Though Harduttrai dealt in a large number of commodities, his strength lay in organizing the market for silver speculation. The silver futures market played a role almost as seminal as the opium, cotton and jute markets (the last during the First World War period). The opium market reached its dizzy heights in the years before the First World War as the trade itself was being shut down as the result of a coordinated international movement to control the drug. Jute reached its speculative heights during the First World War when it was the raw material of choice for sacks used to package gunpowder. Cotton had its speculative apex during the American Civil War (1860–65). Dinshaw Wacha, a talented nineteenth-century Bombay journalist, has produced a classic account of the cotton boom of the American Civil War period which continues to attract attention.[17]

Motilal Jhunjhunwala was to dominate the silver market in a later period. His descendants and protégés are found among India's leading businessmen. R.K. Dalmia, once among India's three largest industrialists, got his start through association with his relative Jhunjhunwala. One descendant of Motilal has a memoir covering Motilal's descendants who are now to be found all over the world, many of them in prosperous circumstances.[18]

The stock market was another focus for speculation. The Marwaris entered the stock market between 1860 and 1900. The Calcutta Stock Exchange was formally organized in 1850. In 1863, a list of stockbrokers shows few Marwari names. By 1900, more than one-fourth of the stockbrokers in Calcutta were Marwaris. Babulal Gangaprasad Soni was founded in 1892 by Babulal Soni of Didwana in Jodhpur who had been a merchant in Mirzapur, but was already dealing in shares in Calcutta in 1872. His son-in-law, Magniram Bangur, arrived later and was a major figure in speculation on coal stocks between 1904 and 1908. Later, the Bangurs became a major industrial business group.

The stock market was closely interrelated with other markets. Many of the major jute shares increased three times in value between 1915 and 1921. The price of a seat on the Bombay Stock Exchange went up from Rs 2900 in 1914 to Rs 48,000 in 1921. The boom during the Second World War was more subdued but the fluctuations were great. Interestingly, while there is some written history of the First World War period in the share market, I am yet to find a good account of the Second World War period in India.

Speculative wealth does have a tendency to be evanescent. It is made in booms and lost in busts, but when the game of musical chairs ends there are always some people seated. Some successful speculators have been so habituated to speculation that their love of the game exceeds their capacity and they lose their stake. This certainly happened to Keshoram Poddar, also one of the first Marwaris to enter the jute industry along with G.D. Birla. Keshoram Poddar (1883–1945)—the grandson of Soniram Poddar, one of the early Marwari traders in Calcutta—specialized in the shares of several mills managed by McLeod and Company. He had started business as a teenager, as an underbroker to Mitsui, the leading Japanese firm in India. Next, he went into the umbrella business, always a good prospect in rainy Calcutta. Finally, he became a sugar broker, especially to Rallis. By 1909, Keshoram was already a prosperous merchant. When the First World War broke out, he became a leading stockbroker. He was one of a small group of Indian brokers allowed to directly deal in hessians and gunny bags with the big British firms. He started to import sugar and cement from Java. He developed close ties with several Japanese firms. He bought heavily into Calcutta real estate, especially blocks of luxury apartments for Europeans built over the last several decades by Jewish and Armenian businessmen. He went into the taxi business, ran ferries on inland waterways, bought a colliery and a flour mill, and loaned the capital to start the Hindi daily newspaper, the *Vishwamitra*. He dabbled in brick kilns, and was rumoured to be cornering the brick market. He bought a jute mill from Andrew Yule in 1918 for Rs 80 lakh. At his height, he was supposed to be worth Rs 3 crore, but his bookkeeping was rudimentary and his approach to business carefree. The reverses he suffered in the post–First World War period finished him.

Baldevdas Dudhwawala had an uncle who entered the stock market in 1880. He and his brother, Basantlal, started in the Calcutta stock market at the turn of the century. Baldevdas specialized in the Kamarhatty Jute Mills Company shares during the First World War period. Reportedly financed by British banks hugely, it is said that he earned Rs 50 crore a year in dividends alone on shares held by him.

Vishveshvarlal Halwasiya (1870–1925) and Hargovindrai Dalmiya, both from Bhiwani, owned the firm Vishveshvarlal Hargovind, an active speculator both in shares and gunny. Vishveshvarlal's father was a jeweller in Hyderabad while his uncle had a leading firm in Lucknow and Calcutta. Hargovindrai's father had established his firm in Calcutta in 1866. The firm Vishveshvarlal Hargovind was formed in 1890. When the firm was partitioned between the partners in 1921 each partner took away Rs 2.5 crore, an enormous sum in those days.

Historically, the greatest speculators sometimes played a critical role in industrial entrepreneurship. The wealthiest in many countries are people whose prime skill is the ability to play speculative markets and manage risk, be it Warren Buffett or George Soros.

Of the leading Marwari businessmen today no one has the public prominence of Rakesh Jhunjhuwala, the Indian Warren Buffett.

If tracing the details of large business group holdings is difficult, the reverse is the case with Rakesh Jhunjhunwala. Just like in the reclusive Warren Buffett's case, Jhunjhunwala's every investment is closely followed by the market and the public, and his results have been astounding. In the earlier years he was thought to be a bit of a bear but is now the pre-eminent bull in the market. Unlike Warren Buffett, he is flamboyant and a bon vivant. Interviewers report his endless cigars, swigging draughts of $400-a-bottle single malt Scotch whisky, his flashy cars, and frank and overtly sexual discourses which call for censoring. However, it should be noted that despite all the innuendos—Jhunjhunwala recently announced that a world-class Mumbai required world-class nightclubs—he is reportedly a devoted family man. Unlike Warren Buffett, his father was not a businessman (Buffett's father was also a member of the US Congress and a leader of the far-right John Birch Society) but an income tax officer and a punter on the stock market who originally sparked Jhunjhunwala's interest.

Jhunjhunwala's public presence is underlined by the fact that he was the pre-eminent billionaire interviewed by the *Financial Times* for its 'Billionaires Club'[19] section in a recent weekend piece on India, was the subject of an entire blog entitled 'The Fake Jhunjhunwala' and was featured in several recent movies.

Though the stereotype of the Marwaris is certainly a puritanical one, there is no question that several of the great speculators of the past were reported to be bon vivants as well, indulging in liquor and prostitutes. So Jhunjhunwala is not an aberration in that respect. This is also the stereotype of speculators in London and New York and has been well documented in bestsellers like Michael Lewis's *The Big Short* and *Liar's Poker* or in fiction like Tom Wolfe's *Bonfire of the Vanities*, to say nothing of a mass of popular and academic writing of a similar kind.

Why Were the Marwaris Successful before Independence?

My academic answers in 1978 (in *The Marwaris*, my earlier book) had to do with psychological disposition (depending on the business concerned different orientations served very well), social support networks and individual and historical factors. This was before 'to network' became a verb, but there were still a lot of commentators (dare I say pandits) who knew how to write 'prose'[20] and referred to networks in various ways. All of these are factors which resonate with the characteristics of the Marwari community, and are shared with other successful Indian business communities. Communities and castes with a history of involvement in business orient their children, traditionally their boys (and now frequently their girls), to the trade, applaud success and know how to help each other in business. It is for this reason that the psychological make-up of those who run businesses in crowded markets is often marked by 'n-affiliation' (a psychological orientation to work social networks, as politicians do), rather than 'n-achievement', which was posited as characterized by Schumpeterian entrepreneurs venturing into new fields (the psychological orientation to launch successful innovative enterprises).[21] In a study of small engineering shop owners in Howrah, Raymond Owens demonstrated that members of the Mahisya caste, who were prominent among owners of shops, had high n-affiliation since their business success was dependent on networking with caste fellows. The other entrepreneurs who came from a wide variety of castes, usually upper-class 'service castes' (Brahmins, Kayasthas, Baidyas), had high n-achievement.

Marwaris from business families were expected to work in and expand their family firms if they had them, to work for others in such firms if they did not, and perhaps to start new firms of their own in due course. Unlike those from 'service' communities they were not expected to qualify in examinations and work for social and governmental institutions. Entrenched in tradition, as a lot of them were, young Marwaris did what was expected of them.

I find, from my experiences, research and travels in Rajasthan and India, that among the young Marwaris I met in 1970, often from humble families in their Rajasthan homeland, many have succeeded well in businesses in India and around the globe.

Everything in the environment of these young Marwari men assisted them in being successful in business. They had a first-class support network constituted by their traditional family firms, business groups and the community. When they arrived in a new place, they found a basa, which provided boarding, lodging and society. Their friends and relatives were often already in business and could help them. Their families guided them in a manner to prepare them for their destined roles.

Because of their earlier positions in the market, Marwari firms found themselves particularly suited to avail opportunities brought about by British rule in the nineteenth century. They also had the benefit of a cultural orientation that directed them towards business. Now that the Marwaris of today can afford the best education and have access to the highest levels of professional advice, they are therefore even better equipped to start businesses.

This book attempts to determine to what extent

these factors continue to play a role even today. Even though we might pay attention to their psychological orientation as a factor when explaining their success, support networks (especially those of the family firm, business group and business community) and specific historical circumstances are still important.

The Modernity of Tradition[22]

When I wrote my earlier book, *The Marwaris*, in the 1970s, there were many people who believed in the polarity of tradition and modernity. Tradition was seen as eternal, unchanging. Traditional Hindu traders, especially those who belonged to the Vallabhacharya Vaishnava and Jain sects (to which many Marwari and Gujarati traders adhere) were not expected to engage in modern economic activity successfully because of the weight of the business traditions they inherited. Max Weber, the great German sociologist, one of the fathers of sociology as an academic discipline, had written as much in *Religion of India*, and his influence was widespread. The concept that traditional Indian merchants were unsuited to modern industry was still current among 'practical' men though experience indicates otherwise. Of course, the 'scribblers' current among practical men are typically those of their youth when they were still open to what the world had to offer. As John Maynard Keynes, in *The General Theory of Employment, Interest and Money*, wrote: 'Practical men, who believe themselves to be quite exempt from any intellectual influence, are usually slaves of some defunct economists. Madmen in authority, who hear voices in the air, are distilling their frenzy from some academic scribbler of a few years back'.

David McClelland, a currently fashionable theorist, in the 1960s stated:

> Probably the most widely accepted general notion that theorists have as to why some nations have developed more rapidly than others is that . . . they are more willing to break with industrial survivals of an earlier period and to accept the social and industrial innovations which are part of the new industrial society.[23]

McClelland, the author of this summary statement, did recognize that entrepreneurs are sometimes the most traditional members of their societies, but he concludes his book with injunctions to increase female emancipation and dissolve family structures in order to increase the amount of entrepreneurship and thus growth in a society.

Traditional traders did become industrial entrepreneurs. They did so as part of the general process of making use of the new, reconciling and combining it with commercial tradition, and sometimes even using the tradition itself to produce a new and more effective synthesis. The process was explained at some length in Milton Singer's *When a Great Tradition Modernizes*, where he described how orthodox Brahmin households in Madras reconciled their traditional social practices with modern economic roles, by processes such as differetiating their lives into Western and traditional segments. *The Modernity of Tradition*, a key book from the 1960s about India, emphasized this aspect.

Traditional institutions like family firms, business groups and business communities are among the leading drivers of entrepreneurship in Indian and many non-Western societies. These institutions and traditional business orientations may be an advantage in many modern circumstances. It is true that traditional institutions can constrain innovation but in business-community contexts they may enable it. Further, as Khanna and Palepu argue, the family, business-group and business-community networks may substitute for the absence of capital markets or modern business technologies. Edward Banfield, deliberating on south Italy, argues that the lack of a joint family system is a key retarder to south Italy's economic progress.[24] The family network was able to overcome the distrust of others (outsiders) which otherwise foreclosed much-needed commercial collaboration.

The use of traditional business tools is not necessarily in contradiction to a paradigm of success in which business schools and MBAs, sometimes combined with a technocratic orientation, provide the basis for support networks, specific techniques and even business legacies, which are required for success. But traditional businessmen are often chary about these. Aditya Birla is quoted as having said:

> I have nothing against MBAs. They are brilliant boys, extremely bright and enterprising. There is nothing wrong with the man, but the training that is given is better suited to multinationals . . . Business institutes unfortunately have a bias for sales and also their whole culture is westernized so they do not really fit in with Indian culture.[25]

As we will see, his heirs are no longer certain on such matters.

*

Why were the Marwaris successful in business and by extension how can everyone else be? I repeated the question to a Marwari friend before a Lions Club meeting I was addressing on the subject of my earlier book, and he said, 'That's simple: marry a wealthy Marwari's daughter', dating the remark to more sexist times.

There is obviously still much general interest in why the Marwaris have been disproportionately successful in business in India.

THE MARWARIS   77

4. THE MARWARIS IN INDEPENDENT INDIA: IN TRADITIONAL INDUSTRIES AND SUNRISE SECTORS

SPECULATIVE KILLINGS ENABLED the accumulation of large amounts of funds which were the basis for new and important enterprises. The Marwaris and other Indians who invested in new industrial initiatives after the two World Wars were businessmen such as the Birlas, the Dalmias and Keshoram Poddar, who had made their money through wartime speculation. The Parsee Tatas' initial wealth and that of many earlier entrepreneurs came from nineteenth-century speculation on opium and cotton. In the debate on the merits and demerits of business groups, their access to pools of capital is taken as a key merit (as it is in the case of venture and angel capital funds).

Of the successful speculators, aside from the Birla and Poddar mills, Harduttrai Chamaria's children set up two jute mills in the 1930s. Hukumchand set up another. Hukumchand also started an insurance company, a steel rolling mill, and added to his chain of textile mills after the First World War. His first two cotton textile mills from 1909 and 1913 were both in Indore. In 1916, he added yet another in Indore and took management control of another mill in Ujjain soon after. Ram Krishna Dalmia went into sugar, cement and newspapers.

Of course, the most dramatic case was that of the Birlas. Kudaisya emphasized that profits from jute and hessian trading, and silver and stock market speculation enabled the rapid rise of the Birla firms. By the end of the First World War, Birla stood second only to Ralli Brothers as a raw-jute and hessian exporter. By 1922, even though most of the jute mills were still under foreign management, Birla, Hukumchand and Halwasiya had their own mills. In 1911, only one significant jute mill had an Indian director, even though Marwaris were reported to already own 60 per cent of the shares in them. And more than half were managed by five European managing agencies.[1]

The first Marwari-owned Indian jute mill faced hurdles in getting land, was charged more for transport and barred from membership by the Indian Jute Mill Association which forced them to use European brokers.

The original Birla Jute Mill had Scottish members on its board and Scottish management, which was gradually replaced as Indians learned the trade.

The Marwaris and Social Change

The emergence of the Marwaris into prominence in the new economy, culture and polity of India in the nineteenth and twentieth centuries posed challenges for the members of the community. They were also identified with efforts to bring about a change in the Hindi language, Hinduism as a religion, and politics. In addressing these issues, there were often conflicts between tradition and modernity that confronted the community, conflicts that the Marwaris continue to face to this day. Again, if one is to surf the Internet to find where the term 'Marwari' appears—beyond horses and languages (Marwari is one of a number of languages which have now been effectively subsumed under modern Hindi)—one finds discussion of the role of the Marwaris in promoting social reform and also, contrarily, resisting it. Recently, in the 1980s, a lot of attention has been paid to the Rani Sati temple in Jhunjhunu, Shekhawati, which is devoted to the memory of a widow who immolated herself on her husband's funeral pyre several hundred years ago. The trustees and others connected with the temple are explicit that they do not propose that modern widows should do likewise. Nonetheless, the temple and the cult connected with it have been the target of considerable protest from social reformers. The temple has been popular as a locus for Marwari children's first haircuts and other rituals for decades. For most Marwaris, the fact that the temple is connected with someone who immolated herself is not a salient feature. In fact, self-immolation was not particularly popular among traders but was more a Rajput custom, even when it was occasionally practised.[2]

The Marwari entry into modern markets and industry in the 1920s and 1930s was naturally accompanied by social change and clashes between reformers and orthodoxy. In the Maheshwari community, the Birlas spearheaded the reform movement on issues such as foreign travel, Western education, especially for women, and the relaxation of restrictions on marriage with members of certain groups that some of the more orthodox wanted to exclude. The caste was divided between their supporters and opponents. But broadly, similar issues divided each caste.

Ghanshyamdas Birla and Jamnalal Bajaj were early and major donors and fundraisers for the Indian National Congress party, though in varying degrees they were opposed by a number of the established banian families.

But when a court case threatened to reveal major secret donations to the Congress by Calcutta banians in 1930, one of the banians committed suicide.[3] The banian approach to this issue was convoluted. G.D. Birla resented racial discrimination in British business houses in India which led him to join the 'terrorist' nationalists, and only family influence eventually enabled him to come out of hiding. On the other hand, many Marwari grandees were, at the very least publically, the epitome of loyalty to the British.

The Marwaris and Literature: Revival of the Hindi Language

The second or third item which pops up while surfing the Web for Marwaris and Hindi literature is the site of the Marwari Library in Delhi which, we are informed, has been striving for the last century, 'towards the cause of promoting Hindi ... worldwide'. Not surprisingly, there are similar libraries in other major cities, including the Rajasthan Club in Calcutta which is a centre for Hindi and Sanskrit activity. In general, throughout the last 150 years, Marwari patrons and writers have been key figures in Hindi literature. Anne Hardgrove in an article focused on younger women Hindi-language writers in Calcutta who document the social transition experienced by their generation.[4] But the

role of the Marwaris in Hindi literature has been noticeable
throughout its modern history.

*

Generally speaking, there is a change among young
Marwaris who have been educated at leading international
institutions and manage enterprises based on new-age
technology. Often, marriages today defy the traditional
caste strictures; quite a few prominent Marwari heirs in
recent times have married non-Marwaris. Young people
are marrying those they work or study with, things that
their elders considered unorthodox and avoided. Also,
divorces have become common as the youth is more
frequently taking its own decisions regarding marriage and
is not tied down by social restrictions. At the same time,
many young Marwaris are effecting social and intellectual
changes in their traditions and traditional approaches to
business. Anne Hardgrave has documented at some length
the transformations and challenges faced by the younger
Marwari women of Calcutta.[5] An interesting book, *Stages
of Capitalism: Law, Culture, and Market Governance in Late
Colonial India*, by Ritu Birla, a professor of anthropology
in Canada, focuses on issues that the Marwari community
has been confronted with. The cover of the paperback
edition of her book depicts the G.D. Birla family tree,
though this fact may not be apparent to most readers.

Obviously, Dr Birla herself is an example of the variety of paths pursued by the present generation of Marwaris.

One aspect of this change is young Marwaris deserting business. It is noted with interest that the ex–railway minister Lalu Prasad's key IAS adviser in his reorganization of the Indian Railways was a Marwari, who chose a career in the Indian civil service rather than entering one in business. Two of the leading politicians of independent India, Ram Manohar Lohia and Kamal Nath, are both Marwaris. No one could say that the rabble-rousing Lohia conformed to any particular Marwari stereotype. Today, there are Marwari doctors, lawyers and professors in large numbers. Not surprisingly, in traditional circles they tend to marry into Marwari business families; in less traditional families, these professional Marwaris often marry people from other communities.

More recently, the process of modernization in the Marwari community has clearly accelerated. It is perhaps notable in the work of Gita Piramal, very much a Marwari lady of the educated generation (a PhD and scion of a leading Marwari family, and on whom I have relied extensively for the purpose of this book), in that she on the one hand notes the emergence of Marwari women in business as in the case of the daughters of K.K. Birla, and at the same time underlines in her writing the residual conservatism of Marwaris families in introducing their women to business.

5. DO THE MARWARIS AND THE BAZAAR ECONOMY STILL SHINE AFTER 1991?

THAT THE MARWARIS played a prominent role in Indian business and industry in the 1960s is not in doubt. At that time there was a flurry of studies describing the continued dominance of large business groups after a decade of 'socialism', or what can be termed as 'industrial licensing'. Both the Kothari and the Monopoly Commission reports attempted to explain the success of big 'business groups' and proposed measures to increase the role of people, who did not come from traditional business communities, in entrepreneurship. In fact, starting from the earliest days of Indian independence there has been a series of extensive government-supported programmes to promote entrepreneurship among communities without a business tradition.

Have the Marwaris been similarly successful in the last thirty years, since the beginning of liberalization? Medha Kudaisya, in her academic biography of G.D. Birla, has a chapter titled 'Business Fortunes in Nehru's India' in which she concludes:

> In retrospect, the Nehru years had seen a major business expansion for the Birlas. Notwithstanding the socialist rhetoric of planned economic development, the Birla business empire continued to flourish. This was due to Birla's strategic vision in which he was fully supported by his brothers and the younger generation. Before independence, the Birla group's share capital stood at Rs 24.8 crore; in 1958 it stood at Rs 68.6 crore. The book value of gross capital stock of public companies more than doubled in these years . . . Together with the Tatas, the Birlas accounted for approximately one-fifth of the physical assets of the corporate private sector.[1]

The Birlas are now represented by a group of different firms, all descendants of Raja Baldevdas Birla. According to *India Today*, they include the following separate business groups:

Sons of Baldevdas Birla	Descendant I	Descendant II	Descendant III	Assets in Crores of Rupees
Jugal Kishore, 1883–1967	Lakshmi Narain (adopted, first son of Ghanshyamdas), 1910–94	Sudarshan Kumar, b. 1934	Siddharth, b. 1957	549.8
Rameshwar Das, 1892–1983	Madhav Prasad, 1917–90			3537.6
	Gajanan, 1910–61	Ashok Vardhan, 1939–90	Yashovardan, b. 1967	864.04
Ghanshyamdas, 1894–1983	Krishna Kumar, 1981–2008	Nandini Nopany, b. 1949; Jyotsna Poddar, b. 1953; Shobhana Bhartia, b. 1957		16,469.6
	Basant Kumar, b. 1921	Aditya Vikram, 1943–95	Kumar Mangalam, b. 1967	83,412.04
Brij Mohan, 1905–82	Ganga Prasad, 1922–2010	Chandrakant, b. 1955		4037.67

Source: Rahman, 'The Big Story', India Today, 5 March 2012.

All Marwaris are not equal to the Birlas, and the experience of the 'Licence-Permit Raj', a term coined by the Indian statesman C. Rajagopalachari, may not be the 'shining' and reformed India of the post-1980s. As Gurcharan Das points out in his *India Unbound*, the Birlas have remained India's largest business group over five generations. This itself probably speaks volumes about what leads to business success.

There are many who are concerned that Marwari and other established Indian business groups were crippled by the several decades of dirigiste government policies and lessened competition in the period between the 1950s and the ushering in of liberalization in the 1980s. Some business leaders, a group epitomized by the Bombay Club, certainly concurred and tried to oppose the liberalization.

The Bombay Club was organized in 1993 in the Belvedere, a 'private' club in the Oberoi Hotel in Bombay, and included leading industrialists. While several of them were Marwaris such as Rahul Bajaj and Hari Shankar Singhania, there were non-Marwaris as well who included Lalit Mohan Thapar, M.V. Arunachalam and Bharat Ram. These proponents of anti-liberalization were opposed by Marwaris like R.P. Goenka, and Shashi and Ravi Ruia of the Essar Group. According to various sources other industrialists too sympathized with them. But who those sympathizers were is not on record.

The members of the club complained that they were unduly handicapped in the process of opening the Indian economy and asked that concessions were to be extended to them. It seemed that a number of the members of the Bombay Club had varying difficulties adjusting to the new Indian economy, lacking access to funds and cash-cow enterprises, and in reorienting their business positions. But others, incidentally, seemed to have done just fine. Some of them felt threatened by the wave of foreign acquisitions; others felt that foreigners were getting Indian enterprises too cheaply. Their key demand was for access to more and cheaper funds.

> Unfortunately, the line between giving Indian industry a fair chance and protectionism was a dangerous tightrope. How much time should the Indian industry be given? In India, the cost of money is higher than in the West and the gaps in infrastructure so wide that the playing field can never be truly equal. There were no easy answers and the Club was criticized as 'a group of inefficient producers fearing competition'. Frightened by the backlash over the next few weeks, several founders backed out discreetly . . . By the close of 1994, 'it was a club of one', says Bajaj ruefully.[2]

The role of business communities is considered at greater length in Dwijendra Tripathi's *The Concise*

Oxford History of Indian Business.[3] He and his co-author, Jyoti Jumani, conclude that Marwaris and commercial communities still play a prominent role, though we will see later that the subject is the focus of some controversy. Even Harish Damodaran in a book devoted to chronicling the emergence of new Indian entrepreneurs from new non-business communities in recent years concedes that, especially in north India, business communities including the Marwaris continue to play a dominant role.[4]

A recent article by Khanna and Palepu of Harvard Business School demonstrates the continuing importance of Marwari and other family-controlled business groups in Indian business. Khanna and Palepu are able to show that the share of family business groups in India as a whole in the ownership of large-scale Indian business is not so different from what it was in 1939, 1969 and 1997.[5] Khanna and Palepu further make evident the fact that such business-group family firms are important in the burgeoning world of information technology also and use this as an argument to support the idea that the mobilization of capital and human resources by business groups is the dominant reason for their continuing importance.

Khanna and Palepu recognize that the specific identity of the leading individual family business groups changes in each period, particularly when one considers those in information technology. What emerges is the stability of the leading Indian business groups. The Parsee Tatas are the largest group in all three years, that is 1939, 1969 and 1997, and groups like the Birlas, Jugal Kishore, Singhanias (J.K. group) and Hariram Goenka remain influential. Some of the groups cited have been partitioned among family members, but as a whole these business families continue to be important.

Of course, some business families have declined and a number of new ones have emerged such as the Ambanis. But the fact is that though the founders of the new information technology groups are sometimes from non-business backgrounds, the list is still dominated by family business groups from traditional business communities.

What the Press Has to Say

The *Forbes* billionaire list of the permanent and the evanescent in business includes a number of Indians residing in India and elsewhere. New Marwaris such as Rakesh Jhunjhunwala and at least two Birlas feature.[6] Interestingly, no Tatas appears on the list though they run India's largest business group. The reason may well be that their funds are parked in trusts (the money abroad is presumably already counted) and their personal wealth is moderate. Other 'rich' lists too are well populated by the Marwaris.[7] It is reported that there are 1,27,000 dollar millionaires in India, constituting 0.1 per cent of the population, as compared to Switzerland where the total number of dollar millionaires constitutes almost 30 per cent of the population, or in the US where they constitute 9.3 per cent of the population.[8] Lest this sound high, note that 1 million dollars of net assets, including a family house, would generate $20,000–30,000 of income in today's America. Retirees are told that the amount is insufficient for maintaining a normal upper-middle-class retirement, even when added to the social security (a maximum of about $39,000) and any supplemental employer-provided pensions they may have. American supplemental pensions vary widely but rarely amount to more than 20–40 per cent of the last-drawn pay.

Clearly millionaires are no longer rare, but a billion dollars of net worth is something more substantial, one thousand times more. My wife once mentioned that a pile of 1 million dollars is a couple of metres tall; a pile of 1 billion dollars is as tall as the towering Washington Monument in Washington, DC—about 170 metres.

Of the forty-six Indians on the 2010 *Forbes* billionaire list, twelve are Marwaris, mostly from old and established families. The non-Marwaris on the list also tend to come from established business families that have been wealthy for two, three or more generations. Some are heirs to large firms who have used their acumen to make them larger. And there are some leading firms that have declined in size over time but still make the cut as far as the list is concerned.

The *India Today* issue of March 2012 carried a section titled 'The Inheritors', the young heirs to major industrial fortunes. Of the twenty-two business groups which featured in the survey, four are prominent Marwari family groups which include two Piramals (related but separate in business), the steel Mittals and the RPG Group. In one Piramal group, three scions head different branches of the group. Harsh, an MBA from London Business School, now manages the group's textiles and auto parts subsidiaries, but it is noted that he worked with India's first shopping mall. Rajiv looks after the group's real estate interests, and Nandan their football club and entertainment business. In the other Piramal group, Anand, a Harvard MBA, and Nandini Piramal, an MBA from Stanford, have expanded the group's health-care business and have invested in several social enterprises. As regards the steel Mittals, Aditya Mittal, a Wharton MBA, is the sole heir. Finally, RPG Group's Shashwat Goenka has completed an undergraduate degree from Wharton. Though it is unclear what he will eventually do, presumably he will head the group in the course of time.

Besides the older Marwari families such as the Birlas and the Bajajs, there are a number of new Marwari billionaires which include Rakesh Jhunjhunwala, the Ruias of Essar and the Dhoots of Videocon.

Not all Marwari firms are resident Indian firms any more. Some are headquartered abroad. The textile group of Shri Prakash Lohia is in Thailand, while the steel Mittals and Bagris are in London. Even the India-based groups often have a considerable global presence. And not all contemporary 'Marwari' groups are purely Marwari any more. Intermarriage with other communities means that the actual heirs sometimes come from different backgrounds.

Why Are the Marwaris Still Successful?

Traditional business firms like the Marwari ones flourished both in the period of the Licence-Permit Raj lasting into the 1980s as well as the period of liberalization which followed thereafter. It is not surprising that success in one period leads to success in the next. As the adage goes, the best way to make a million dollars is to start with a billion.

During the period 1950–80, it was alleged that the ability of established business groups to influence government decisions in obtaining industrial investment licences, which determined who would be permitted to start industry, was a major advantage.[9] Pranab Bardhan writes:

> The corrupt grip of the corporate oligarchy in Indian political life and state allocation of access to land, monopoly rights on natural resources, or telecommunications, is much too evident. As fighting elections becomes more expensive, it is not uncommon to see a large number of wealthy people among new legislators, and the generally rising role of donations, often under the table, by companies (and increasingly real estate businesses) to election funds.

Ashutosh Varshney and Jayant Sinha in a recent article in the *Financial Times* distinguish between entrepreneurial and 'robber baron' capitalists, in the context of Indian business, who owe their success to corrupt government and anticompetitive market practices.[10]

Pranab Bardhan's hypothesis that the predominance of business groups is primarily a result of their ability to manipulate the bureaucratic and political process may not hold water. Though many of the leading business groups were frozen out of licences during much of this period, they grew in various forms. Political involvement, 'trust in princes', is a two-edged sword. This is dramatically illustrated in Gita Piramal's *Business Maharajas* where in her survey she observes that among the most vigorous, successful and innovative business entrepreneurs in both periods, many had been frozen out of the licensing process for long periods. She reports that Rahul Bajaj was blocked almost continuously, as was Aditya Birla after 1977. Rama Prasad Goenka and Brij Mohan Khaitan did better, but they primarily acquired existing firms rather than engaging in greenfield activity requiring licences.[11] If a limited number of licences were to be awarded among a large group of competitors it was only natural that the decision-makers would take into account the track record of applicants and tend to award the licences to those who were already large-scale operators. Further, given the financial and managerial resources that the concerned business groups possessed, it is no surprise that they were able to, in different ways, evade the licensing restrictions—investing abroad with borrowed money, for example. This is very much what the Tatas and the Aditya Birla Group did. Or else, business groups would combine with those who were able to secure licences and often ultimately ended up taking over the licences completely for themselves.

In the period following the onset of liberalization, it is alleged that the established business groups exploited their existing oligopoly dominance in different industries to exclude new entrants.

One account reports:

> Closer examination does not suggest a story of dramatic transformation (in the patterns of industrial ownership) following liberalization, but rather one of an economy still dominated by the incumbents (state-owned firms and business groups). The exception to this pattern is the growing importance of new and large private firms in the services sector. Sectors dominated by state-owned and business group affiliated firms before liberalization . . . remain so following liberalization.[12]

It is also said that traditional business groups unfairly exploited their positions through 'tunnelling' and 'propping' and otherwise exploiting certain enterprises under their control to support others. This will be debated at greater length when discussing business groups, but it should be pointed out that while there is indeed reason for concern as regards minority shareholders from many a point of view, the losses for them are greater than for the economy as a whole which is likely to be benefited, at least in the short run.

The merits of these allegations need to be addressed empirically, but leading firms as a whole, such as the Birlas, tend to focus on their bottom line and thus prove beneficial to their shareholders. It is hardly likely that these firms engage in 'industrial sabotage'.

6. WHAT PRODUCES BUSINESS SUCCESS: LESSONS LEARNED

Family Firms, Business Groups and Business Communities in India and Abroad

IN THE SECTIONS that will follow we will define and consider three institutions in the Indian context as well as in the context of several contemporary contentions—family firms, business groups and business communities.

Indian businesses, especially those owned by traditional business communities like the Marwaris, are typically family firms, they are frequently organized in the form of 'business groups', and the families that own them are frequently members of business communities. These institutional forms and their evolution were seen as reasons for Marwari success in the early period, and for relative failure later.

Family Firms

Family firms are common everywhere in the world. Even in the United States some of the largest firms are 'family owned' and some have remained in the same family for generations. In the US, family firms account for 35 per cent of all firms. In Standard & Poor's 500 list they account for 95 per cent of firms, 50 per cent of production and 42 per cent of employment. In Germany, they account for 80 per cent of firms as also for 60 per cent of the national product.[1]

Some of these family firms have achieved longevity. We are informed that the Birlas are now in their seventh generation as a large business group, and the Rockefellers and Fords have had a significant presence in the American economy over a similar span. An article reveals a list of firms founded before 1800; the oldest is a temple construction firm in Kyoto dating back to 578 CE. The list features a number of familiar names with interests in vineyards, construction and banking, including the Japanese Kikkoman Soy Sauce Company which goes back to 1630.[2] This list of firms is obviously incomplete; it misses out several old Indian firms going back to the seventeenth and eighteenth centuries.

There is even an association of firms going back to before 1800 CE known as the Henokiens (after Henok or Enoch, a name coming from the Bible), which has a number of European and some Japanese members and an active website, www.henokien.org. The comparable British Tercentenarian Club does not have a website but is active. The relative presence and importance of family firms in the Indian private sector is high, and their persistence, as family firms, high as well. The secretary of Henokiens, Lipovitch, indicated to me that the association would very much like to have Indian members.

There is a group of originally German Jewish family firms (Greek and Armenian ones as well) which were key factors in international trade and finance for decades. There is an interesting story about how some of these have fared over the last several turbulent decades in financial markets. The British historian Cecil Roth argued in his book on the Sassoons that their commercial continuity was enabled by their adhering to ethnic traditions.[3] It is for this reason that the descendants of those branches of the Warburg and Rothschild families that survive as commercial entities have remained Jewish. Many of the other leading Jewish banking families converted to Christianity and no longer have independent commercial presence (for example, the Bleichroeders, Schröders, Mendelssohns, Itzigs, etc.).

However, the fate of European international banks is a complex topic which calls for a book of its own. Literature exists on these primarily Jewish bankers to German rulers and how they became key funders of international trade in the nineteenth century. Literature also exists on how their descendants assimilated into the general international upper class. The British have a saying that 'the coach rarely passes the church door for three generations'. Many successful British businessmen were Quakers and other types of dissenters and 'passed' the door of the official Anglican Church to go to their own chapels or meeting houses. A remarkable number of their descendants joined the Church of England.

What it means for a family firm to 'exist' is a complex question in pre-corporate economies. The firm and the family are identical. The family may have been in business for generations. And all families, it is asserted, go back equally far—to the beginnings of mankind.

Whether family firms are a good thing and whether they are successful is a more controversial topic. A flood of literature establishes that founder-run firms are most efficient.[4] The situation with family firms otherwise is more murky. In general, the literature in the US and some Asian countries suggests that they are less successful than professionally managed firms.[5] Data from Europe and perhaps elsewhere suggests the reverse.[6]

Allan R. Cohen wrote a classic but now hard-to-find book in 1974, *Tradition, Change and Conflict in Indian*

Family Business, which was based on eight Harvard Business School case studies on Indian family firms, at least three of which appear to be Marwari.[7] He came to the not surprising conclusion that where the business firm and the family structure represented and accepted the same family hierarchy (senior/junior) it worked, and where there were conflicts, it did not. These case studies also documented the extent of the conflicts. Some would say that they occurred more, and probably so, because of contemporary social changes in Indian society as a whole. But these kinds of conflicts between family and business necessities have been endemic in the Indian family and family firms from time immemorial, though undoubtedly the social sanctions for the family hierarchy itself have weakened in present times.

The Birlas as a Family Business

The Birlas, together with their numerous offshoots, are collectively the largest Marwari business family group and India's second richest. Many members of the Birla family have published autobiographies from which I quote extensively in this book. Most have emphasized the importance of accounting skills, cautious and centralized financial control along with parsimony in expenditure, as the secrets to their firms' success. Operational autonomy for professional managers is important. Conversely, the decline of other family firms is sometimes attributed to loose financial control and the inability to sustain operational autonomy for executives. These are, of course, precisely the features that characterized the Great Firms. These also cover careful succession planning and training of heirs which successful business family firms like the Birlas practise. The relative success of the Birlas in retaining their money has been partially attributed to their successful handling of succession and transition. Finally, the autobiographies deal with the role of family firms as venture capitalists, identifying and investing in the best ventures at any given time. There is obviously an element of convention in all these autobiographies (or sometimes authorized biographies) but the business memoirs are clearly sincere and validated by many outside observers.

Kudaisya in her biography of G.D. Birla highlights certain values which are even more basic and fundamental than the characteristics emphasized in the memoirs. She begins with what is assumed in the autobiographies with regard to religious orthodoxy and subordination of individualism to the family—the essence of tradition. She continues:

More significant than learning . . . skills was the inculcation of the family's code of business in the young initiates . . . it was merely an extension of the code of restraint they had been taught at home . . . the reputation of the family was most important since the community had reposed full faith on us. Even if a single enterprise failed, the blame would fall on the entire Birla family.[8]

In what follows are issues involving family business success and continuity, which often rise to the conscious level as businessmen reminisce on their professional lives.

Challenges for Marwaris Family Businesses

Factors in the accounts of the Birla business success indicate how they overcame various challenges.

The Importance of Proper Accounting Systems

Says K.K. Birla:

To run a business successfully, one has to be well versed in accounts. Ever since the days of grandfather, every member of the family understood accounts well. It was felt, and rightly in my opinion, that a man with a comprehensive background of accounts could not be cheated in business.[9]

The 'Parta' System

Father [Ghanshyamdas Birla] . . . started the famous

parta system of accounting for which our family and our organization have acquired fame. Father developed the system with such finesse that it could provide a daily profit and loss statement on the performance of the unit concerned.

B.K. (Basant Kumar) Birla, K.K.'s elder brother, gives a similar account in his biography.[10] Gita Piramal in her account of Basant Kumar's son, Aditya Kumar, reports:

Under BK's supervision, Aditya acquired a meticulous knowledge of accounts, particularly the parta, the centuries old traditional Marwari system of monitoring and financial control. Though its use was widespread among Marwari firms in the nineteenth century, most gave it up gradually. Today, it is almost unique to the Birlas who use it extensively. In the late '80s, Aditya convened a conference of his top executives from all over the world to discuss the parta, and compare it with other systems. By the end of the conference, he realized that through it the group was saving Rs 100 crore.[11]

According to Siddharth Birla, one of Aditya's nephews: 'This system has many advantages. Essentially it emphasizes the speed of reporting, even sacrificing some accuracy in the process. There is mental pressure on the manager to perform daily'.

Uncle Ganga Prasad Birla says: 'The family widely adopted the system during the depression years. Money was tight, credit was not easily available, and you had to worry about money more than anything else.'[12]

Given this, it is interesting to note that the Aditya Birla (G.D. Birla's grandson) Group, now run by his son, Kumar Mangalam, gave up the parta system in 2003 for the 'Cash Value Added' method of reporting results. It was reported that the parta concentrated excessively on production, while the Cash Value Added method looked equally at profitability, asset productivity, and growth.[13] The change was part of a more general change in orientation which will be discussed later.

The Need to Decentralize in a Large Organization

K.K. Birla reports:

I believe in decentralization. Once I asked Pandit Govind Ballabh Pant, when he was chief minister of Uttar Pradesh, how strong his hold over the administration was. He said, 'Krishna Kumar, not a leaf in my state moves without my approval'. What he said was correct. The state did not move, whereas the rest of India moved forward.[14]

Or perhaps more revealingly:

> Once R.K. Dhawan, Indira Gandhi's assistant, sent for
> me. He said that the prime minister wanted two students
> to be admitted to BITS (Birla Institute of Technology
> and Science at Pilani, Rajasthan). I explained the position
> to Dhawan and expressed my helplessness in the matter.
> I felt it was fruitless to discuss further as he was only
> carrying out directions given by the prime minister. I
> requested Dhawan to fix an appointment for me with
> Indiraji to allow me to explain the position to her . . . I
> explained the position to Indiraji, who appreciated it but
> asked me an exploratory question '. . . can nothing be done
> in the matter?' I said, 'Indiraji, there is a simple solution
> provided you accept'. I told her that I was prepared to
> place five seats at the disposal of the prime minister. These
> could be regarded as the prime minister's quota. My only
> stipulation for the quota would be that the recommended
> person should not have obtained less than a certain
> percentage of marks, say 70 per cent. On this basis, the five
> students would be accepted. At the same time I also said,
> 'Indiraji, for these five seats you will receive 500 requests
> for admission'. Indiraji smiled and said that I was a clever
> man to have passed the buck to her.[15]

A leading Kolkata industrialist of the present generation
(a decade or two younger than K.K.) once said that his
enterprises did well when he left them to his trusted

executives. Whenever he intervened they got into trouble. The decline of several leading business families from several decades ago is generally attributed to too much intervention by the family members and not enough delegation to professional executives.

But we should not assume that the only role of the family firm is to delegate, as explained in the final sections.

Limits of Delegation and the Strategic Role of the Family Centre

Gita Piramal quotes Shashi Ruia, another industrialist: 'The key to Aditya Birla's success lay in his ability to organize himself and everyone around him'. She proceeds to quote Birla himself: 'What do you do to attract people? You give them tremendous powers and independence while monitoring their performance'. Aditya's tight management team, consisting of mostly Shekhawati Marwaris like himself, was well regarded, though it has almost fully been replaced by his son, Kumar Mangalam.

Delegating control to executives is not a panacea. One notes the phrase 'monitoring their performance' in the quote above. The story of the revival of the Tata group under Ratan Tata's leadership is partially a story of his bringing to heel powerful executives who had developed too much autonomy under his predecessor, J.R.D. The difficulty is to preserve a distance from details. As Aditya Birla says, 'Watch the financials, intervene if necessary, decide what next industry to get into, and which ones to withdraw from'. The story of the rise and decline of Indian family firms and groups is partially one that details which firms have managed to spot the prospects as they unfold and which stayed with old, declining industries.[16]

Hence, once the system is in place, a business group needs to make the right entrepreneurial start-up decisions.

Choosing the Right Enterprise

The ideal Indian family business group is similar to other venture capital firms or wealth managers but in contrast to its Western counterparts, it, more often than not, takes the initiative rather than wait for entrepreneurs. If anything, this bias towards taking the initiative has now been facilitated by the spread of management education which inculcates skills for evaluating new investments in terms of increasing stockholder value and the members of family groups have learned them formally.

The Birlas Scout Out New Opportunities

K.K. Birla deals with this issue in terms of the first enterprise he worked on—the creation of an Indian textile machinery company. This was a task which he found most unpromising:

> Father's thinking was that as the textile industry was the most developed industry in the country at that time, the manufacture of textile machinery should prove to be very profitable . . . I thought to embark on this venture without proper knowhow would be a rash and hazardous undertaking. At any rate, as father had already decided, we had to proceed with the project and there was no looking back . . . There is a big difference between a consumer industry and a capital goods industry. In a consumer industry, like textiles or jute goods, there is a market even for products of inferior quality . . . if the design and workmanship of capital goods are not up to the mark, that becomes a permanent headache for the customer. This is what I tried to explain to father. He did not agree with this view. I, therefore, made frantic efforts to find a suitable foreign collaboration.
>
> . . . In reply, father gave me a lecture on what could and should be done. I had no doubt in my mind that what father was saying was of academic significance and to venture into the manufacture of textile machinery alone was like striking one's head against a wall. Uncle BM (Brij Mohan Birla), as I mentioned earlier,

was more practical. He entirely agreed with me and discussed my problems with father.

We get a somewhat similar account in his brother B.K.'s autobiography:

One day, towards the end of 1937, Kakoji (G.D. Birla) out of the blue told me, 'Basanta, your college career will end in March, 1938. You will have to give your full time to business after that. I have arranged for you to enter into medicine manufacture. I have engaged a foreigner, Mr. Percs, for this scheme. He is a specialist in hormone medicines. He will be in Calcutta in March or April, 1938. I will arrange a meeting with him. I have specially selected this project for you. It's a new field; you will have to work hard'. That was all and then he changed the topic! It was done so casually that I felt a little nervous.

I had no idea what hormones were, how much investment would be required to set up the factory, what the sales possibilities were, from where I would get a manager, and so on. My mind was in a whirl. After all, I was just seventeen and a college student. One more thing to keep in mind, a seventeen year old Birla boy of today is altogether different from a seventeen year old Birla boy of those days. Television, computers, comics, foreign travel and schooling from the age of two onwards make today's children mature much faster than they did in those days.

A few days later, when I wanted to discuss this new scheme with Kakoji, the reply I got was, 'We will talk about it when Percs comes'.[17]

B.K.'s account does not give details of the ultimate result. As reported by Kudaisya, Jugal Kishore, B.K.'s pious uncle, vetoed the whole operation despite its profitability because it involved using animal products.[18] It turns out that as with textile machinery, there were a few hiccups in this business start-up process too.

Looking for the next sector to invest in is not alien behaviour. Those who remember Dustin Hoffman's performance in *The Graduate* remember the older friend who whispered 'plastics' in his ear as the direction of success. The same is echoed in K.K. Birla's quote about how the family directed him, mistakenly he thought, into textile machinery, or B.K.'s discussion of hormone medicine.

Securing Succession and Continuity

The greatest challenge to the survival of a family business is connected with succession, ensuring that the family members from each succeeding generation are able to manage the firm successfully. Often firms dissolve either because of conflict among family members or because of their incompetence. Conversely, family firms face difficulty in inspiring the loyalty of non-family members whose skills may be needed.

To meet these challenges, founders of family businesses embark on a serious programme of education for their heirs. In K.K. Birla's biography, which details his experiences following the completion of his undergraduate studies (which he did eventually as a private student in Hindi), we are told that he then studied accounts:

Within six months, I had become proficient in accounts . . . Father thought that if I acquired some knowledge of the technical side of the workings of a textile unit it would stand me in good stead in managing the textile business. He selected Panchu Babu to give me lessons on the technical side of a textile unit. A south Indian, Panchu Babu was the cost accountant at the Kesoram Cotton Mills. He was neither a technician nor did he have any accountancy background. He was, however, an able man and had a good knowledge of both accountancy and the working of a textile unit . . . What Panchu Babu taught me was the theory of spinning, weaving and sizing.

. . . Father then sent me to Jiyajeerao Cotton Mills at Gwalior which was one of the best managed units in our organization. Not only that, late Durgaprasad Mandelia, who was the most senior manager under my father, was in charge of this mill. I stayed in Gwalior in 1939 for three months and got thorough training under

Durgaprasad . . . In Gwalior, I got training in stores, timekeeping and the technical side. I learnt the names of hundreds of items used in textile mills, such as shuttles, bobbins, picking band, temple, weft fork holder, lease rod, drop box pickers, weft pern, reed hields, not to speak of items which are used in every factory like bolts and nuts, screws, files, etc. Durgaprasad asked me to try to remember who the important manufacturers of important items were, what was the volume of their consumption, what their rates were, and all other details. Not only that, to give me a thorough grasp of the technical side, he asked a fitter to open a carding engine, which is an important machine in a spinning unit, to teach me the names of each part and then to reassemble the carding engine in my presence. I could not have found a better guide.[19]

This was all in the 1930s but the pattern would not be too different today, except that an MBA from a leading international business school and perhaps a technical degree in a field of interest to the family business would be expected from the heirs. Aditya Birla, G.D.'s grandson, was one of the first to acquire an engineering degree from MIT, and his son, Kumar Mangalam, is an MBA and a chartered accountant.

Part of the conventional autobiographical account is usually the proposition that 'Father was correct and far seeing'—as in the supposed Mark Twain comment that when he was eighteen, his father seemed the dumbest man in the world, but by the time he was twenty-one it was remarkable how his father had matured.[20] The narratives indicate that paternal guidance is not always perfect, as is seen in the statements of K.K. and B.K. Birla. Kudaisya asserts that G.D. Birla, their father, was so focused on public affairs that he did not share the kind of relationship with his sons that his brothers (B.M. and R.D.) did. An advantage of the extended family is that if the needed rapport is absent with one relative, it is often there with another.

The specific factors mentioned give a general idea of behavioral patterns in family firms especially those that are at the centre of business groups. They monitor and evaluate; they allocate capital and managerial resources. Generally speaking, they perform a strategic but not a tactical role. But they also face some inherent challenges connected with social, as distinguished from commercial, sustainability. There are a variety of answers to these challenges—right and wrong—and they are connected with a range of management styles.

Management Styles: Fathers and Sons—Intuition and Systems

There are different styles manifest in how the heads of

Marwari firms handle the challenge of intervention in their groups' day-to-day functioning. Piramal lays in contrast what she sees as the highly rational analytic style of Aditya Birla and Rahul Bajaj with the more intuitive style of B.M. (Brij Mohan) Khaitan and Rama Prasad Goenka; she implies that Goenka's heirs and successors practiced a more rational style. She quotes Rama Prasad Goenka as having said:

> I hear that my sons are more comfortable when they have figures before them, but I have always preferred to listen to people. My gut feeling is my only pathfinder. Harsh, like Ratan Tata, is conscious of and worried about the need for structured planning and appears to be concerned about his father's enthusiastic response to every opportunity that comes his way.[21]

Some of these differences in style between fathers and sons reflect the idea that those who found businesses and those who inherit them are bound to have different professional approaches. Even in non-family firms, like Apple and to a lesser extent Microsoft, tension between the founders and the managers of routine innovation is observed.

Typically, it has been seen that founder-managed family firms outperform non-family firms, whereas heir-managed family firms do not. However, this is not the case everywhere. All Japanese family firms, whether run by heirs or founders, outperform others, and incidentally the highest performers are those managed by adopted heirs—quite frequently, heirs who have attained their status by marrying into the family.[22]

Piramal focuses her attention on her two paradigms, the inheritors of large groups, Rahul Bajaj and Aditya Birla, emphasizing the importance of the strategic vision that they brought to their groups (as she does with Ratan Tata) in sharp contrast to the intuitive style of many of the business founders. The inheritors as distinguished from the founders in her vision are more systematic and organized. The heirs are also characterized as being more attentive to quality issues, though this may be an adaptation to the greater competitiveness of the Indian market today. Aditya Birla's son, Kumar Mangalam, replaced his father's senior executives, changed the financial reporting system, and more importantly changed the human resources system, responding both to his own style and the changing demands of business in post-reform India.

Each new generation might be expected to bring in new ideas. The heirs of a business house might differ from its founders. They might feel a compulsion to address problems which they feel had been accumulating as the founder aged and times changed. The changes brought by Ratan Tata were as dramatic as those brought by Kumar Mangalam Birla. If the retirement of old executives moved more slowly in Tata's case there were reasons everyone understood. These reasons were rooted in the ethic of the Tata group and the relationships its senior executives had with the companies. Gita Piramal reports similarly that Harsh Vardhan Goenka commissioned a McKinsey study which recommended various changes, and though his father felt that these changes were dubious the RPG Group still went ahead and implemented them.[23]

One of the greatest challenges family businesses face is the 'routinization of charisma'.[24] Undoubtedly, entrepreneurs can found and manage businesses using their intuition. For an institution, business or otherwise, the founder's charisma has to be institutionalized. This is obviously what heirs strive to do but it is difficult.

Nassim Taleb points out in his latest bestseller, *Antifragile*,[25] that business school techniques and theories should be derived from successful business practice, not the other way around. It is to be expected that successful business practitioners may not need them, but their heirs might value the systematization and explication business schools provide. Taleb reports a business economist telling him that to handle a particularly complex financial derivative one had to know the Girsanov theorem. But

none of the traders he knew had ever heard of such a
thing. Given their proclivities he felt they would think
it a brand of vodka! Or as Wassily Leontief, an economic
quant, said once: If you cannot explain something in
words it is false, even if a mathematical explanation
is often more concise, easier, and certainly more
computable. In a more generalized way, the intuitions
of successful business founders obviously worked for
them; their heirs might prefer tried-and-tested methods.

The Birla versus the Tata Style

Piramal describes the Birla style, focusing on loyalty
and financial control, as recognizable enough, so it
leads foreign firms, disposing of their assets, to prefer
a B.M. Khaitan or a Rama Prasad Goenka with a less
uniform and more relaxed style of management. But as
we shall see, defining that style is not so easy. To quote
Piramal again: 'While a Tata success depended on the
performance of individual executives, the Aditya Birla
group depended on its systems'. That is all very well,
but as we find later in her book she thinks that the Birla
success depended as well on the strategic vision and the
organized pursuit of it by Aditya Birla as an innovative
entrepreneur engaging in continuous, systematically
planned, and rapid expansion. In fact she has a later quote

from Aditya Birla in a specific reference to Ratan Tata—
one which is more generally applicable: 'If you don't have
systems, any individual will fail, and if you have systems
but don't have a leader to lead the system, it will fail . . .
I'm sure the Tatas have very good systems'.[26] What Aditya
Birla may not have recognized is that Ratan Tata was also
hoping to have a system for innovation that transcended
individual leadership. Whether that was achievable was
the issue. Tata thought that he needed to change his
companies' attitudes to respond to competition and serve
customers more efficiently than they did. Piramal quotes
Aditya Birla: 'I think there is a need to take some hard
decisions which doesn't come from guidance alone . . .
Success is knocking confidence into Ratan'.[27]

Problems of an Exclusively Financial Focus

The social sustainability of an enterprise is more than
a commercial question. Just as the success of business
groups is connected with scanning the horizon to see
where to put funds next, failure is connected with staying
rooted in declining fields, markets and technology.

The 'brand' of a business group is critical and that is a
matter of the group's management systems, core values,
and specific charismatic leaders. Thus, a business group
needs accounts and good investment policies, but it also

needs the less tangible aspects of a brand even for its own commercial purposes. Beyond that, businessmen like to think that they are accomplishing certain moral purposes in the world, and for that they need their brand even more. Whether capitalism is moral or a matter of morality is a controversial issue, but it is clear that many of its successful practitioners would attest to capitalism being a moral endeavour.

There is thus a limit to a purely financial approach to entrepreneurship. One problem is the term profitability, which is extremely short-term in nature. Financial return maximization needs to be tempered by a broader concern about the social and corporate culture aspects of new investments, and Indian business groups with a family as well as a financial rationale are ideally placed to consider long-run and contextual factors. No Indian businessman will be unaware of what his peers think of him in the context of a continuing business family with a 'brand', an intangible that has value and needs to be cherished.

Kudaisya's analysis, referred to earlier, about the importance of prior moral values in the success of the Birla style is just one example of how the brand stems from family and community style and underlies the systems of a successful firm.

There is a large reservoir of anthropological literature

on the cultural and social implications of standard financial management and economics and the need to transcend it for business to survive and flourish.[28] Henry Kaufman and Warren Buffett posit that a pure financial management approach ignores two other considerations. The first is the extent of the prevalence of commercially relevant factors that are not fully captured by financial data alone. An excellent example for this are the problems American Express encountered when it acquired Edmond Safra's bank, which had a different commercial culture from its own. Years ago, an American Express executive said to me sniffily, 'We lend on what is recorded in the books.' Compare this to the Bank of Credit and Commerce International (BCCI) which considered many less explicit factors in its lending relationships. The business philosophy of the Safra bank was based on long-term understandings with clients, many of them operating in countries where transparency requirements would have put an end to their activities. The acquisition failed at a considerable cost to the transactors. Later when HSBC bought the bank, and it had to be bought as there were no Safra family heirs though other Safra family members remained in business, HSBC carefully managed the corporate cultural areas. The Middle Eastern cultural ambience of many of Edmond Safra's clients did not meld easily with the proper 'white shoe' approach of American Express. The other aspect is the extent to which individual maximization of financial value may be inconsistent with the system maximization of value for all parties—the kind of issue we face after every major financial system–centred crisis. These problems are faced by the economy as a whole as well as individually by each firm and business group.

All of this is in addition to the fact that short-term financial success may undermine long-term commercial sustainability. This may not be a prime concern for salaried executives who can move on, but is ever present for family enterprises which intend to continue to trade under their brand.

Dealing with Non-Family Executives: Delegation as a Strategy

The problem of employing and working with non-family executives or technicians who are critical to the business is central to the success of the firm. The Birla group has often been rated well because of its ability to inspire loyalty among these executives, though admittedly many are distantly related or at least members of the broader Marwari community. But Kudaisya states:

[In the] style of management within Birla businesses,

kin-based and loyalty have always remained the byword. It has been well recognized that top managerial positions were held by Marwaris and only by those close to the Birla clan. This has delayed the professionalization of management of many of their firms.[29]

The Birlas, and many others as well, also prosper when they use non-Marwari, and now sometimes non-Indian, executives. A number of the early key Birla executives were non-Marwari, as indicated by the names observed in the various family memoirs. A traditional way to handle this conflict between professional and family management was to have the executives marry into the family. This is not a strategy unknown to family firms elsewhere. The first non-DuPont head of the DuPont family firm was Greenewalt, a son-in-law. It is also possible to enable the executives to become heirs by founding their own family firms, and this has certainly been the case for the Birlas.[30] Several large business groups today were founded by former or sometimes serving Birla executives. Finally, Hindu families like the Marwaris have the custom of adoption, usually from allied families, if there is a lack of male heirs. Karen Leonard in her recent work on the leading business families of Hyderabad—Marwari, Gujarati, Goswami and Muslim—shows how several used this practice.[32]

Adoption is a time-honoured practice in Hindu law and is widely used. Nominally, it secures an heir to perform the funerary rites, but in practice permits the commercial sustainability of the family. Even though adoption is common among large Marwari firms—Ghanshyamdas Birla's eldest son, Lakshmi Narain, was adopted by his elder brother, Jugal Kishore; Motilal Jhunjhunwala adopted his brother's eldest son—there seems to be no data on its effect on business continuity.

US data is explicit that inheritor-managed firms do poorly when compared to those managed by outside professionals, though incidentally the former do better if the quality of the inheritors' education is 'better'. The European experience seems to indicate the reverse, while the Thai experience is more like the US. What the situation is in India is still a subject of considerable debate.

Resistance to Succession Strategies

Often, some heirs simply refuse to enter the business and replacements are necessary. The matter is perhaps easier in Europe and in the US, where businesses can easily be sold and the proceeds managed by trusts or other institutions. In the US, trusts created in the nineteenth and early twentieth centuries still handle the large funds which many of the leading wealthy families accumulated.[32]

In other cases, the problem is not that the next generation is not willing to enter the business. Defying wealthy parents is not unusual—passive resistance is more common. But the question is how to handle children who are not competent, and are reluctant to recognize their limitations. The challenge for a young heir is not to efface himself (or, progressively, herself) so much that he is discounted, and also not to assert himself when professional executives or even technicians are more competent.[33] Gurcharan Das quotes Rahul Bajaj: 'It is easy to get rid of an outside manager, but how do you get rid of a family member? You must either do what is right for the business or the family. Either way, you will end up with an angry family or a weak company'.[34]

Family Conflict

Even when the next generation is willing and capable, conflicts are common among brothers. To counter this possibility family firms are often very carefully partitioned during the founders' lifetime.

Formulas for preserving a family firm unit are a subject of great discussion. Gurcharan Das emphasized equity among members of the family but this is extremely difficult to deliver. The generalization, as cited in Allan R. Cohen's case studies for Harvard Business School for the 1970s, is probably accurate: where the family hierarchy is congruent with the business hierarchy things work; where it is in conflict they do not.

In some cases, no formal separation was required because the family was already legally divided as with the members of some business groups referred to below. On the other hand, the wrangle between the two Ambani brothers, where a harmonious partition was not arranged, has been in the public domain and harmful to both their groups.[35] More dramatic is the story of the Birlas in the case of G.D. Birla's nephew, Gajanan, who refused to comply with family strictures and was made to distance himself from the family in 1935. The issue was deserting his wife. She and her sons, Ashok and Yashovardhan, continued to be very much a part of the family and their heirs own one of the significant Birla successor firms. The children from Gajanan's second marriage have generally been out of the limelight, but reappeared in the court litigation over the M.P. (Madhav Prasad) Birla estate.[36] However, the bigger story has to do with the partition before and after G.D. Birla's death.

Kudaisya raises questions about the success of the Birla partition.[37] But what she actually reports is that the complex nature of interlocking stockholdings meant that issues continued to come up and were successfully negotiated between the various branches of the family after G.D.'s death in 1983.

Gita Piramal describes the tensions and bitterness between the different Birla groups, especially during the 1983–96 process of separation. Sudarshan Birla of the C.K. (Chandra Kant) Group felt he had received too small a share, and some adjustments were eventually made in his favour, but the adjustment was not sufficient according to Piramal to satisfy Sudarshan Kumar and his uncle K.K. (Krishna Kumar), who had only daughters. Further, a number of K.K.'s units had been nationalized. Piramal gives the following quote from Aditya's father, B.K.:

> After 1983, it was clear that unless some kind of division was agreed upon, there would not only be problems in the course of time but also misunderstandings and even unpleasantness. At the same time there was, I think, some hesitation in all four of us about how to start discussing the division.

Piramal reports that initially it was only G.D. Birla's heirs who were concerned, but eventually their cousins too became involved. To be precise, besides G.D.'s grandsons, Aditya and Sudarshan, their two first cousins too were involved, although Ashok, who died in a crash in 1990 leaving everything to his young son Yashovardhan, refused to contest the matter.

The Birla division was finalized at some financial cost to all concerned but particularly to the Aditya Birla Group (who the others thought had emerged with a disproportionately large share).[38] Gita Piramal estimates the cost to Aditya and his father as about two billion rupees. In 1987, there were differences about Upper Ganges Sugar, a company predominantly owned by G.P. (Ganga Prasad) but managed by his nephew Aditya. The Calcutta Stock Exchange had to step in, as it did with respect to Sutlej Cotton (primarily an investment firm, despite the name). Though the Sutlej Cotton conflict did not involve Aditya, it did G.D.'s other heirs. But the moot point is that by 1996, the process was finished.

To quote Piramal:

By May 1996, a power sharing formula for Century Textiles, the last festering sore, had been worked out. Nobody was completely satisfied but at least workable compromises of sorts had been achieved and the clan would stop breathing down each other's necks.[39]

It is hoped that the Ambanis too have ended their feud and arrived at a compromise.

A less commercially significant but untidy trail of events surrounded the death of M.P. Birla's widow in 2004, when it was found that she had left his large estate (estimated to be around Rs 500 crore) to a trusted personal adviser. Though the case was contested in court, the adviser remains in possession of the assets concerned.

The problem of partition goes with having a family firm. An intriguing study of the Filipino Ayalas, one of the leading business groups there, describes some of the negotiations that were involved in their evolution which read much like those of the Birlas.[40] Even Friedrich Engels, the co-founder of Marxism, was involved in complicated negotiations cutting him out of the family firm which provided much of his and Karl Marx's economic support during their lifetime.[41] I was recently involved with publishing a set of business cases about intergenerational continuity in Nigerian family firms, some of them of Indian ethnic origin; such a study reveals the same difficulties faced by some Indian family firms and the same mechanisms employed to overcome them.

Anand Saxena in an article titled 'Succession in Indian Business Houses' argues that the succession issue is the one on which Indian firms have most typically foundered and argues for careful succession planning. However, much as such planning might be desirable, circumstances often frustrate it.[42] Hence, exceptions aside, most family businesses hold together for at most a couple of generations after which divisions often presage their decline.

Random Factors

Gita Piramal has published a series of books (*Business Maharajas*, *Business Legends*) in which she analyses the styles and reasons for the success and failure of several large industrialists she has studied, many of them Marwari. She emphasizes individual and specific family characteristics, financial management, planning and organization. As it happens, the selection of new enterprises often turns out to be influenced not only by rational analysis but also by specific family circumstances. Khaitan's controversial (both from a commercial and policy viewpoint) acquisition of Union Carbide India was motivated partially by a desire to find a vent for their son Deepak, who they were worried was much too interested in his racing-horse stable.[43] The decision by Rama Prasad Goenka to acquire CESC, the Calcutta utility company, was motivated by a need to have an enterprise for his son, Sanjiv, after the family lost the firm, for which he was formerly responsible, to an outside partner.

Other decisions of this kind were motivated by personal ties and conflicts among India's elite business families which emerge as the various players get into continuous contact with one another. The conflict between the Bajajs and Firodias for Bajaj Auto is well documented, as well as the complex interactions between the Italian Piaggio firm and the Agnellis of Fiat.[44] Significant are the interventions by other more 'senior' industrialists to deter hostile takeover efforts launched by B.M. Khaitan and Rama Prasad Goenka. When Rama Prasad Goenka launched a takeover effort for Bombay Dyeing, it was J.R.D. Tata who convinced him to desist, and similarly Goenka abandoned an effort to take over Premier Autos because of 'peer pressure'.[45]

The Web gives us a rambling article titled 'The Rise, Fall and Rise of Indian Business Families', covering thirteen Indian families of which four are Marwari.[46] The Birlas and the RPG Group are reported to have maintained themselves, the steel Mittals have, of course, increased their span of business, while the Singhanias have declined. However, it is perhaps too facile to assume that the conclusion drawn by the said article is definitive because the Satyam family group, one of the rising groups, ran into trouble later. It is also to be noted that the Thapar group (non-Marwari) about which the author of the article is quite critical seems to have produced an heir who has been getting excellent reviews. The article ascribes the decline to family feuds, poor management and lack of industrial focus. It does not mention, as it probably should have, the luck factor of a group being in either a sunset or sunrise industrial sector. To quote King Lear, 'who's in, who's out' keeps changing. Some heirs go into decline while there are others who revive their groups.

While each of these factors may be critical there could be exceptions. Generally speaking, after US business firms were ripped apart by the antitrust authorities some entities post separation performed better—for example, Standard Oil Trust and the phone monopoly AT&T. In contrast, some entities have experienced a worsening of performance after merging with others. It is not clear why the same cannot apply to Indian firms, except that often different firms within a business group are so closely interlinked that separating them proves difficult. Nonetheless, one of the key strategies to sustain a business group is often dividing the operations between family members. In fact, one study reveals that Indian family firms which underwent succession fights did better than those that did not, even though splits per se were negative, but the methodology is so complex that many people will not be convinced that having a succession fight could prove to be a good thing for a family firm.[47] Undoubtedly, unfocused groups can have problems, but the logic of a conglomerate or private-equity operator, etc., which specializes in overall management, has continuing attraction. Of course, poor management will always spell decline.

Business Groups

Indian firms are typically parts of family business groups and loosely affiliated with one another, sometimes through interlocking stockholdings or boards of directors but frequently with more informal ties.[48] These business groups are also typically family controlled, in a few cases by more than one family.

Several Indian business groups have tried to achieve a kind of 'post-family' cohesion. The Sarabhais attempted it, in an effort documented in management literature.[49] The Sarabhai experiment did not work. The entire history of the Sarabhai group is a classic Indian business story which is still to be fully documented. The Birlas seem to have done better by retaining executives and handling family-property divisions successfully. The cohesiveness of the Tata group, which is at least three generations old, is presumably a success and at the moment Ratan Tata has passed the reins on to the next generation. The Tata family has continued to play a predominant role. Finer cases involve the transition from British management to professional Indian management (Larsen & Toubro, ITC and Bird-Heilgers) but even in these cases it is not clear how permanent the settlements will be.

Business groups are found in many developing countries and management experts attribute their success to the groups' ability to mobilize capital and management resources despite the lack of well-organized markets as also to their competence in managing complex interactions with the government and other partners.

Professors from Harvard Business School, like Khanna and Palepu, and the handbook of practical businessmen, the *Economist* of London, speak in favour of highly diversified conglomerates:

Most emerging countries have a penchant for highly diversified conglomerates. India's Tata Group, which accounts for almost 6% of the country's G.D.P., has subsidiaries in carmaking, agricultural chemicals, hotels, telecommunications and consulting . . . such diversification is not confined to giant organizations. China is full of small and medium-sized companies that have fingers in many pies . . .

. . . In their different ways . . . these corporate forms are creative responses to their circumstances . . . Diversified conglomerates can adapt to environments rife with political and financial risks.[50]

The article goes on to quote Khanna on business group advantages in accessing capital and managerial talent.

The Tata Group can use capital from established businesses to support growth in new ones, and has the resources to attract and train the best people. It can also use its brand name to sell all sorts of products. Indians who have grown up enjoying Tata tea might be more inclined to buy the latest Tata electric car.

. . . The Tata Group reckons that its brand is worth about 100 billion rupees ($2.2 billion).[51]

More generally, business groups and communities can generate substitutes for a number of missing elements including capital and management markets, and also legal systems. To quote an account of contemporary developments in China:

The networks and institutions that develop around informal economy clusters may be based on ties of kinship, community or geography. Their social function is to provide information about opportunities, start-up support and a network of trust that ensures sanctity of contract. Promotional organizations run by the state and the norms set by formal laws are but a poor substitute for these institutions, particularly in countries where enforcement of norms is weakened by widespread corruption and judicial tardiness.[52]

Business groups are a universal phenomenon, but especially prominent in India. The positives are that they are able to make up for missing markets by putting together capital and managerial ability where others cannot. In Korea, the *Economist* of 11 February 2012 reported that there was a 'Korean discount' on company value which it attributed to the bad reputation of the Korean *chaebol*, family business groups, on account of the same things discussed in the Indian case—propping, tunnelling, political influence, etc.[53]

But others argue that the negatives are that Indian businesses are poorly managed and attribute this to several factors, all connected with their being family business groups. One is the lack of competition in the markets they face. A second difficulty is the limited delegation of authority. A third criticism has to do with their lack of industrial focus. The best groups are, however, as well managed as any firm in the world.[54] Whether there really is a generally lower level of productivity in Indian industry is actually hard to say. Some studies have shown that multinational corporations in India are not necessarily more efficient than Indian family businesses. But the larger problem is that Indian wages and markets are still so poorly aligned with international ones that relative productivity is hard to compute.

Other Complaints about Business Groups

Another claim is that business groups may enjoy corrupt access to political influence and abuse the enterprises they control for the interest of their controlling group rather than their shareholders. Indian business groups are alleged to 'tunnel' assets out of one firm they control and use them to 'prop up' others. This might not be in the interest of minority shareholders but the level of dissatisfaction is not high enough to deter them from investing in these firms. This conflicting set of approaches has produced an entire cottage industry, in Cambridge, Massachusetts, which is trying to use empirical data to resolve the question on the prevalence of tunnelling and propping. The volume of academic output is impressive, the pyrotechnics with which data is manipulated reasonably sophisticated, and the results not so conclusive that any of the contestants have retreated.[55]

For those less interested in the techniques of data manipulation—no one can deny that successful business groups often have been able to launch successful enterprises where others could not, sometimes almost certainly because of their market credibility and access to capital, as also because they were good entrepreneurs and managers. On the flip side, large businesses often benefit (and sometimes suffer) because of their political connections, and controlling shareholders and managers frequently run the business to benefit themselves, rather than for the benefit of the other stakeholders in their enterprise.

One of the most difficult legal conundrums is defending the interests of shareholders, especially minority ones, without depriving the management of its inherent autonomy and responsibility. The problem is that there are no really good ways to do this. I recollect being summoned late one night to meet a group of the informal 'nomenklatura' (originally a list of strategic party and state officers with certain privileges) who typically controlled ex-Soviet 'oblasts' (districts), and were trying to devise methods to protect minority shareholders in the newly privatized factories in their district. I quickly photocopied some pages from *Company Law in a Nutshell* (a simplified text for US law students) which outlined how weak the best protections were.

The exact empirical balance of what Indian business group managements do is complex. A reputation for treating shareholders poorly would eventually come back to haunt a business group, a consideration probably exacerbated when we are dealing with a family group where descendants are likely to be doing business for several generations and be concerned about their 'brand'. There is no question that business families themselves take some pride in the manner they treat their shareholders. One of the unpleasant techniques employed in bargaining with a family firm is always to say something like 'I know some people do things like this, but I am sure that a family firm with your reputation would not think of doing this', or even stronger reprimands like 'Would your late father/grandfather have done anything like this?'

Almost fifty years ago, I had used this very technique successfully in getting back a rental deposit on a bicycle in Varanasi.

Further, staying with the specifics, one of the counter studies puts the following forward:

> We find that business group affiliation continues to generate higher market valuation vis-à-vis stand-alone firms ten years into the transition (Post 1991 reformed, 'shining' India), but diversification is not the source of these benefits. Instead, we find that propping through profit transfers among firms within a group (including 'tunneling') and better monitoring through group level directorial interlocks explains the higher market valuation of business group affiliated firms.[56]

There is no question that 'propping' should positively affect some group firms and negatively affect others, and consequently affect the interests of shareholders in the propped and tunnelled firms. But the effect on the group's firms as a whole should be positive. Exactly how directorial interlocks will cause higher market valuation independently is not quite clear. One would have thought the fact that the groups are providing good managers to be a virtue rather than a fault.

Is Community Still an Important Factor?

The Shining India of the last few years, after the end of the 2 per cent per capita Hindu rate of growth, has not been a product solely of the 'business communities' but has witnessed the flowering of educated young entrepreneurs who come from varied backgrounds, probably and most commonly what would have been described as 'service' or 'warrior' or 'cultivator' communities. The business communities are still among the leading firms, often doing well, but the service communities are right there with them. Nonetheless, not surprisingly, the business community members still dominate the scene. Business success is ultimately determined case by case; individual firms are competitive and do well. The matter becomes more difficult when we try to explain why certain categories of firms, business groups, business communities, industries and even countries do well by providing the best environment for firms.

There have been discussions on the phenomenon of emerging entrepreneurs and many works documenting the variety of communities from which successful businessmen come. Harish Damodaran's *India's New Capitalists: Case, Business, and Industry in a Modern Nation* has an introduction from Nandan Nilekani of Infosys who himself is certainly a poster child for successful entrepreneurs from non-business communities.[57] This lively and well-researched volume by an accomplished economic journalist documents the extent to which entrepreneurs in the last two decades have come from non-commercial communities. The volume does not purport to be comprehensive nor does it assert that non-commercial communities were absent from enterprise earlier. In fact, it makes the point that non-business communities have always been more prominent in the south of India, and attributes this to several factors including the relative weakness of business communities in the areas concerned. For instance, Damodaran argues that in the Coimbatore region 'peasant' communities were able to emerge in textiles and engineering but did not emerge in the southern area of Tamil Nadu where foreign and business communities dominated the cotton trade, the major industry in the area. Damodaran's statement that the princely Rajputs are not prominent as entrepreneurs is surprising, since with their resources and education the more aristocratic Rajputs are major players in a variety of sectors, especially in hotels. As one former maharaja is reputed to have quipped, 'We've been entertaining people for free all our lives, we might as well be paid for it.' It is true that Rajputs have also been closely associated with other entrepreneurs. The tie-up between the Jaipur royal house and the Tata-owned Taj Hotel group included the royals handing over the management of some of their palaces; also, at one point, many of their relatives and more particularly their sub-feudatories worked in the Taj Hotel chain. Other Rajputs have enterprises in different areas.

The success of the Rajputs in the emerging tourist industry of Rajasthan is documented in a study by Lloyd and Susanne Rudolph, 'From Landed Class to Middle Class: Rajput Adaptation in Rajasthan'. To borrow a quote from the study, 'A credible heritage-hotel Rajput identity combines being a believable lord of the manor with being a successful businessman.'

In present times, we recognize that often in the world economy leading industries fall under the service sector—television and radio, health and education, research, legal services, outsourcing. It is therefore not surprising that the groups that are in this sector have hugely benefited. The lines differentiating services, trade, industry and even cultivation have become blurred in the modern economy and it should not be surprising that those involved in entrepreneurship in these different sectors of the economy interact with each other as well. Not only Rajput princes but also leading sportsmen and film actors have emerged as entrepreneurs.

Non-commercial groups have never been absent from the ranks of Indian entrepreneurs. Dwijendra Tripathi's *The Concise Oxford History of Indian Business* records a number of different origins for entrepreneurs over the last several hundred years, such as the Sikhs (Indra Singh from Jamshedpur in engineering), and the Kayastha Srivastava Group in Kanpur, not forgetting the Brahmins and Nadars of south India.

Sometimes these entrepreneurs were restricted to certain industries—the Jatavs and Muslim Quraishis to leather, castes traditionally connected with toddy tapping like the Nadars, Shahas and Kalols to alcoholic beverages, and Mahishya to engineering shops in eastern India. In other instances, Khatris from the Punjab and even Brahmins in Tamil Nadu and Bengal, despite being 'service' castes, have been prominent entrepreneurs in their respective regions for centuries.

Incidentally, Muslims from Shekhawati have also been active in the construction business in Bombay and the Middle East.

Michael Porter in his classic book, *Competitive Strategy: Techniques for Analyzing Industries and Competitors*, on competitive advantage describes a 'hexagon' of factors that facilitate competitiveness, not only for firms but also for industries, countries and, by extension, business groups and communities. Different elements in the social infrastructure empower different entrepreneurs.

Today many of the cogs of infrastructure that traditional Marwari businessmen had to painstakingly create are available to everyone—off the shelf. Those daily accounting systems permitting real-time control and response, once an item of Marwari pride, have now been replaced by continuous online accounts using off-the-shelf softwares. The rapid communication of business news which necessitated carrier pigeons for the Rothschilds or mirror signals for the Birlas is now facilitated by the use of Bloomberg and cellular phones. The Marwari basa in which Marwaris could sleep and eat has been replaced by hotels and restaurants. However, the traditional factors still seem to work.

Sometimes what is important for contemporary entrepreneurship are connections in academia and in the technology community, with the bureaucracy, and links to the financial markets or even access to market chains. Though the Marwaris still have many of these resources, others have acquired them as well.

Now there are the new castes like the old-boy network of elite schools and colleges, the children of elite civil servants and corporate managers, and the armies of MBAs which also provide supporting networks for business opportunities.

The categorization of successful business groups in terms of their community affiliation is only one approach to studying them. A great deal has been written on this approach by me in my 1978 book, *The Marwaris*. Other approaches have included regional approaches such as the areas around Calcutta or Bombay. To reiterate, Damodaran reports different paths to entrepreneurship—from the market for business communities, from the office for service communities and from the field for peasant communities. He even expects powerful surges from among the Dalit communities.

There are rebuttals to the community argument. There are those who attribute Marwaris success in eastern India, and in particular Kolkata, to a strong disinclination towards entrepreneurship among the Bengali elite. However, in places such as Chennai and Mumbai, despite a Marwari presence local business groups have been dominant.

7. CONCLUSION: WHAT ARE THE MARWARIS LEFT WITH?

AT ONE LEVEL nothing has changed. The heirs to the quintessential great Marwari firm of Tarachand Ghanshyamdas are the Poddars and Neotias, leading contemporary entrepreneurs; the heirs of Sir Hari Ram and his son Sir Badridas Goenka, leading banians of yesteryear, have engendered the very successful RPG Group; and the Birlas, the largest group of Marwari speculators to emerge after the First World War, are still among the largest industrialists in India. Two of these three feature in the *Forbes* billionaire list. And the enterprises from which they now draw their prime economic sustenance are not those of the old economy.

Even the new Marwari groups and billionaires evolved in a somewhat comparable fashion. Perhaps large-scale commodity-trading firms are now less prominent (though ethnic Indian firms are prominent among the world's leading commodity traders), and the banian relationships of the colonial days are history, when the foreign partner had direct access to the autocratic government.

Nonetheless, there are business lessons embodied by earlier Marwari businessmen which are still valid and perhaps will remain so.

Watch the Money

There are two key functions performed by the Marwari business firms and business groups—strategic management of investment funds by moving them to where they are most productive in the long term and close financial monitoring of the enterprises in which they have a share. It is perhaps the changes in Harsh Goenka and Kumar Mangalam Birla's business styles that point to a dilution of finance-centric strategies in present times.

Delegate but Monitor

Successful businessmen have to learn how to delegate, otherwise the span of economic activity they can engage in will be limited. They also have to know when to intervene, fully aware that a decision to intervene is costly. Usually it is easier to replace an unsatisfactory executive rather than turn him around. Ineffectual executives and family members are gently moved out to cushy and uncritical positions.

Plan but Have a Style and a System

This is somewhat ambiguous as we clearly see a transition from an intuitive style to a more systematic one. However, this may be, as some suggest, a product of the transition from business founders to inheritors.

Lead to Expand and Do Not Let the System Inhibit Growth

A key characteristic of successful businessmen, as Aditya Birla said in his perhaps inappropriate criticism of Ratan Tata, is a drive to expand. Many firms have expansion in their mission statements but few implement it.

The Right Corporate Culture

The firm or group must have a style which befits its market and the times. Changes or adjustments constitute one of the most difficult tasks. Corporate culture in a firm is critical in inspiring loyalty, especially of competent managers about which commentators like Tarun Khanna are so concerned. Financial incentives can go only thus far, and are sometimes counterproductive.

Don't Get Blown away by Fads

The shelf life of half the management fads is six months. Professors, including those from business schools, devise striking and attractive theories which bear no responsibility for success. A responsible manager has to be more tentative and experimental in his approach. As any school debater knows, there are usually at least two sides to any question, even multiple sides as in the Anekantavada of Jain logic. The problem is to decide which is right in a given situation.

Do Not Miss New Developments

Some businesses describe themselves as 'knowledge businesses'. As a matter of fact, all are. The world's oldest family businesses have had some very successful ventures and a lot of failed ones because of missed opportunities.

AFTERWORD

Do We Know More Today Than We Did in 1978?

My earlier book, *The Marwaris* (1978), was based on existing secondary material, census data, contemporary newspaper sources and primary material, and also used the account books of one of the nineteenth-century Great Firms of Tarachand Ghanshyamdas, kindly provided by its heirs, and a database of over eight hundred family histories which were contained in a series of caste handbooks published in a small town in central India, mostly in the 1930s.

Since 1978, popular and academic 'scribblers' have been active, and we need to ask what they have added to our knowledge.

Many businessmen, among them Marwaris, more

sophisticated and globalized with their degrees from US Ivy League colleges and their equivalents elsewhere, have committed their thoughts on business success to paper, and we should learn from what they have to say.

What is striking in the case of India is how little they talk about business. The businessmen's memoir volumes deal extensively with the political, social and even cultural involvements of successful businessmen. Some of them are critical and analytical, to a greater or lesser extent. However, the space devoted to the details of business in their texts is limited. Perhaps, the most forceful business biography in India is Prakash Tandon's autobiography, now available in a one-volume edition.[1] This volume recounts the experiences of one of the first Indians to become a chartered accountant, and then a chief executive in a multinational firm (Unilever's Indian subsidiary). His tenure at Unilever was followed by his post-retirement experience in managing two gigantic parastatals, the State Trading Corporation and the Punjab National Bank. Like many professional managers, Tandon did not come from a business family but from a service background. As a professional manager in a multinational and later primarily in parastatals, Tandon was certainly not a traditional businessman.

Among traditional business community members, K.K. and B.K. Birlas' recent autobiographies and the biography of their father G.D. Birla by Medha Kudaisya give important insights into how large Indian family firms function.[2] The Birla volumes are only part of a wave of business biographies, many of which contain interesting insights on the inner workings of large firms. So many of these concentrate on the Birlas that to follow family threads and identify numerous family members scattered over generations is difficult.

A lot of academic literature exists on family firms and a significant amount on Indian family firms. Some of this literature is historical and biographical in nature and recounts the experiences of particular firms and family members. A partial list of this literature is available in a bibliography prepared by N. Benjamin and N. Rath at the Gokhale Institute in Pune.[3] However, as explained to me by Alan Thrasher, the South Asian specialist at the Library of Congress in Washington, business biographies are often privately printed and do not get included in the normal bibliographical reference systems.

Aside from this academic and biographical literature, as far as I can tell, there isn't a lot of narrowly construed 'business literature'—novels and films on business subjects—though it is not entirely absent. For example, Satyajit Ray's *Mahanagar* deals with one sort of business; the businessman is frequently characterized as a villain in

Indian cinema. There is also a popular theme in Indian cinema in all the regional variants (Bollywood, Tollywood, etc.)—that of the honest businessman trying to protect his commercial honour while surrounded by thieves.

Two of Chetan Bhagat's bestsellers—on call centres and marketing—certainly deal with particular business environments.[4] If Sankar's comparable novels in Bengali have a less national exposure, that is not due to a lack of quality.[5] Bhagat and Sankar's novels might be considered an Arthur Hailey, James Michener or Tracy Kidder phenomenon—novels which describe a particular economic and social reality for their audience. These are not usually considered business literature. In contrast to literature from other countries, such books are few in India.

Surprisingly, there exists an enormous amount of Japanese business literature, novels and biographies where the plot or subject is primarily business-centric.[6] Japanese business novels really concern themselves with commercial issues. Taichi Sakaiya is concerned with predicting trends and deals with people who recognize and seize the trends. Takeshi Kaikō, in a business novel, though that is not his preferred genre, deals with the complexities of marketing consumer products—in his case, better packaged sweets. Other authors deal with matters at the level of central banks deciding on currency strategies, or businessmen dealing with the problems of dissident shareholders or key customers. But these again really debate on the subject of what is good for society in general, rather than what is good for a business. The criterion differentiating 'business literature' from other genres is that it is written from the viewpoint of the entrepreneur or firm, rather than the society as a whole.

Yet a larger volume of research about family businesses and business groups is produced in forms other than biographies or even novels. Business schools, and business management as a discipline, have produced vast studies and case studies dealing with the advantages of family firms and the specific challenges they face in reconciling their family and business rationales. Academics, after all, must publish or perish.

In addition to all this recent literature, I draw shamelessly on my own earlier research; let me make my apologies for borrowed thoughts, references and even language from my 1978 book. Since my earlier book on the Marwaris was more academic than the present one, I frequently omit my original references—those who are interested can refer to the original.

NOTES

I. Preface

1. K.K. Birla, *Brushes with History*, 83ff.
2. Markowitz, *Merchants, Traders and Entrepreneurs*, 238–39. See also Wikipedia, 'Bhaiband', en.wikipedia.org/wiki/Bhaiband and Wikipedia, 'Lohana', en.wikipedia.org/wiki/Lohana.
3. Damodaran, *India's New Capitalists*, 8–41.
4. Tod, *Annals and Antiquities of Rajasthan*, 166.
5. See Parson, 'The Bazaar and the Bari'.
6. *Census of India 1931*, 529. The 1931 Census was the last attempt at consolidating an accurate collection of caste and community figures. Post-Independence India has been reluctant to encourage casteism. But even before the British stopped their caste enumerations a competitive politicization of the census process by competing communities was undercutting its validity.

   As the 1931 Census report states: 'Of the 846,811 persons born in Rajputana and enumerated elsewhere, the majority in all probability came from Marwar, Bikaner, Jaipur, Jaisalmer and Mewar, but above all from Marwar and Jaipur, and consists of those traders, with their dependants, who are known indiscriminately as Marwaris and play such an ubiquitous and important part in commerce and banking throughout India.' (*Census of India* 1931, 68.)

This is obviously higher than our 3,00,000 estimate, and the detailed rationale appears in Timberg, *The Marwaris*, 107–24, as well as a detailed plotting on the basis of various data primarily from decennial censuses which document the timing of migrations and the sort of enterprises Marwaris were involved in in each region.

7. The 1921 Census reported 6,27,000 merchant-caste members in Rajasthan, forming 6 per cent of the population there. The 1961 census shows roughly 3,00,000 people born in Rajasthan but located elsewhere in India; this figure does not count the many Rajasthanis born to the diaspora but does count those from non-merchant communities. A more detailed census analysis is available in Timberg, *The Marwaris*, 84–90.

8. Yang, *Bazaar India*, 199ff.

9. Tewari, *Business Communities and the Freedom Struggle*, 22–35.

10. 'Rank of Cities on Sanitation 2009-2010', Press Information Bureau, May 2010.

11. Wacziarg and Nath, *Rajasthan*.

12. From the Lal Niwas Hospitality website. Available online at http://www.lalniwas.com/contactus.php.

13. For lists of these, see Tewari, *Business Communities and the Freedom Struggle*.

14. Hardgrove, 'Sati Worship and Marwari Public Identity in India', 723–52. The Jalan connection is specified

in the article since Rani Sati herself was a Jalan; the Tulsian connection is one that I have frequently been told about.

2. The Beginning of the Bazaar Economy

1. Ray, 'Asian Capital in the Age of European Domination', 449–554.
2. Sinha, 'Introduction', v–xxiii.
3. Little, *The House of Jagatseth*.

3. The Marwaris, the Bazaar Economy and the British Raj

1. Cohen, 'Tradition, Values and Inter-Role Conflict in Indian Family Business'.
2. Timberg, *The Marwaris*.
3. Milman, 'The Marwari', 29.
4. Hopkins, 'Ancient and Modern Hindu Guilds', 169–205.
5. *Bengal Hurkaru*, 10 May 1834.
6. See references in Timberg, *The Marwaris*, 140.
7. Sharp, *Good-Bye India*, 18–20.
8. Das, *India Unbound*, 108–10.
9. Misra, *Business, Race, and Politics in British India, c.1850–1960*, 7–11, 57–59, 105, 109–12, 126–32, 194–95, 198.
10. There were several large Baghdadi Jewish firms, and though their families intermarried they were quite separate families. Most of the larger Jewish firms eventually shifted their headquarters to London and sold their Indian

interests. As the ever-quotable Sir Victor Sassoon said, 'I gave up on India, and China gave up on me.'

11. This is because a part of the letters were taken from Germany to Russia by the Soviets and only made public after the end of the Soviet Union—and because they have only recently been translated into English from Western Yiddish, a language now largely dead.

12. Ritu Birla, *Stages of Capitalism*, 143–98; Hardgrove, *Community and Public Culture*.

13. *Gazetteer of Bombay Presidency*, 66–67.

14. *Bajranga Lal Kedia v. King-Emperor*, All India Reporter 1921, Calcutta, 719; *Thakurdas Mundra v. Emperor*, All Indian Reporter 1930, Calcutta, 637, India Cases 128 (Calcutta High Court), 330.

15. Edwardes and Campbell, *The Gazetteer of Bombay City and Island* vol. 1, 299–300.

16. The late Dr Anand Chandavarkar found this reference for me.

17. Wacha, *A Financial Chapter in the History of Bombay City*; Krishnan, 'Bombay Cotton'.

18. Jhunjhunwala and Bharadwaj, *Marwaris: Business Culture and Tradition*.

19. Crabtree, 'India's Billionaries Club', *Financial Times*, 16 November 2012.

20. The French playwright Molière describes an uneducated businessman who is proud to discover once he has the time that he has been writing 'prose' all his life unwittingly.

21. Owens and Nandy, *New Vaishyas*. The terms themselves come from McClelland, *The Achieving Society*.

22. Singer, *When a Great Tradition Modernizes*; Rudolph and Rudolph, *The Modernity of Tradition*.
23. McClelland, *The Achieving Society*, 178.
24. Banfield, *The Moral Basis of a Backward Society*.
25. Piramal, *Business Maharajas*, 195.

4. The Marwaris in Independent India: In Traditional Industries and Sunrise Sectors

1. Kudaisya, *The Life and Times of G.D. Birla*, 45.
2. Hardgrove, 'Sati Worship and Marwari Public Identity in India'.
3. Interview with Prabhudayal Himmatsinghka, Calcutta, 1971.
4. Hardgrove, 'Hindi Literature as a Political Space', 804–06.
5. Hardgrove, 'Community and Public Culture'.

5. Do the Marwaris and the Bazaar Economy Still Shine after 1991?

1. Kudaisya, *The Life and Times of G.D. Birla*, 336.
2. Piramal, *Business Maharajas*, 128.
3. Tripathi and Jumani, *The Concise Oxford History of Indian Business*, 155–81, 234, 235.
4. Damodaran, *India's New Capitalists*, 312.
5. Khanna and Palepu, 'The Evolution of Concentrated Ownership in India', 283–94.
6. See 'The World's Billionaires', *Forbes.com*, 2010.

7. See 'India's Top 100 Richest', available online at www. sophia-ajz.sulekha/blog.post/2009/11/india-s-top-100-richest-52-billionaires-48-millionaires.

8. 'High Net Worth Individuals', *Economist*, 26 June 2010.

9. Bardhan, 'Notes on the Political Economy of India's Tortuous Transition', 31–36. On the other hand he accepts the benefits of liberalization: 'The reforms have unleashed a great deal of hitherto pent-up entrepreneurial energies, and . . . particularly the private corporate sector is now much more vigorous and self-assured in facing global competition and holding its own'. The focus of Bardhan's piece is on the countervailing political forces for economic equity that have also been unleashed.

10. Sinha and Varshney, 'It Is Time for India to Rein in Its Robber Barons', *Financial Times*, 6 January 2011.

11. Piramal, *Business Maharajas*.

12. Alfaro and Chari, 'India Transformed?', 22.

6. What Produces Business Success: Lessons Learned

1. Talreja, 'Succession in Indian Family Firms', 3.

2. O'Hara and Mandel, 'The World's Oldest Family Companies: Convincing Evidence that Smaller Firms Usually Outlast Larger Ones'. The second oldest is a Japanese inn started in 718 CE, the third a French vineyard (which seems like more of a museum) founded in 1000 CE, and the Barone Ricasoli wine and olive operation near Florence dating to 1141 CE. Among names that people may recognize are the Sumitomo Corporation claiming to

have been founded in 1630 CE, the Kronenbourg Brewery (1664 CE), Taittinger Champagne (1734 CE), the Jose Cuervo tequila company (1758 CE), Waterford Wedgwood china (1759 CE), Faber Castell pencils (1761 CE) and Bass Pale Ale (1777 CE). It seems that a number of the listed family firms like Cadbury Schweppes (1783 CE) have ceased to be family firms in recent years. Absent from the list is M.M. Warburg founded in 1798 CE, perhaps because of the Nazi association in its family connection.

3. Jackson, *The Sassoons*, 168.

4. These matters are discussed threadbare mostly with regard to the US in Bertrand and Schoar, 'The Role of Family in Family Firms', 73–96. This is a review article on previous studies in many different countries but it does not directly challenge the proposition—it only argues that family firms are correlated with trust. Also see Barontini and Caprio, 'The Effect of Family Control on Firm Value and Performance'.

5. Barontini and Caprio, 'The Effect of Family Control on Firm Value and Performance'.

6. Bernard and Schoar, 'The Role of Family in Family Firms'.

7. Cohen, *Tradition, Change and Conflict in Indian Family Business*.

8. Kudaisya, *The Life and Times of G.D. Birla*, 194; B.K. Birla, *A Rare Legacy*, 80.

9. K.K. Birla, *Brushes with History*, 41.

10. B.K. Birla, *A Rare Legacy*, 27ff. He also reports being steered by his uncle as a thirteen-year-old when he was encouraged to start investing in shares: B.K. Birla, *A Rare Legacy*, 25–26.

11. Piramal, *Business Maharajas*, 189.

12. Ibid.

13. Datta, Kausik, 'Kumar Mangalam', *Business Standard*, 19 September 2005.

14. K.K. Birla, *Brushes with History*, 313–14.

15. Ibid., 282–83.

16. See Khanna and Palepu's account of how the Tatas have with consistency correctly selected industries to invest in. Also see the excellent documentation on the development of their enterprises in Benjamin and Rath, 'Modern Indian Business History'.

17. B.K. Birla, *A Rare Legacy*, 27.

18. Kudaisya, *The Life and Times of G.D. Birla*, 195–96.

19. K.K. Birla, *Brushes with History*, 83ff.

20. This idea belongs to the considerable realm of Mark Twain oral traditions and is not precisely traceable.

21. Piramal, *Business Maharajas*, 258.

22. Wiwattanakantang, 'Are Japanese Family Firms Successful?'.

23. Piramal, *Business Maharajas*, 256–59.

24. The phrase is Max Weber's.

25. Nassim, *Antifragile*.

26. Piramal, *Business Maharajas*, 403.

27. Ibid., 407.

28. For some consideration of this problem, see Ho, *Liquidated* and Zaloom, *Out of the Pits*. These anthropologists of financial markets and their predecessors ranging back to the great Walter Bagehot strive mightily, often with limited success, to understand the moral outlook of participants in the New York, London and Chicago markets.

29. Kudaisya, *The Life and Times of G.D. Birla*, 395.
30. The Mandelias and the groups of the Khetans and Kanorias are all examples.
31. Leonard, 'Family Firms in Hyderabad', 827–54.
32. Goodwin, 'How the Rich Stay Rich'. Technically, what is involved is not a trust because of the Statute of Perpetuities, but a special form of corporation.
33. Knowledge@wharton, 'The New "Right-Hand Men"'. See also Cohen, *Tradition, Change and Conflict in Indian Family*.
34. Das, *India Unbound*, 266.
35. Leahy, 'Ambani Brothers Agree Peace Deal,' *Financial Times*, 24 May 2010.
36. Kudaisya, *The Life and Times of G.D. Birla*, 192, 195
37. Ibid., 394–95.
38. Piramal, *Business Maharajas*, 164–74.
39. Ibid., 173.
40. Batala, 'Zaibatsu Development in the Philippines', 18–49.
41. Hunt, *Marx's General*, 209–10, 237–38, 261.
42. Saxena, 'Succession in Indian Business Houses'.
43. Piramal, *Business Maharajas*, x–xi, 300–07.
44. Ibid., 229–32.
45. Ibid., 223–24.
46. 'The Rise, Fall and Rise of Indian Business Families', available online at http://www.businessandeconomy.org/14122006/storyd.asp?sid=641&pageno=19.
47. Talreja, 'Succession in Indian Family Firms', 29.
48. Wikipedia, 'Corporate Groups', en.wikipedia.org/wiki/Corporate_group.
49. Rice, *Productivity and Social Organization*, 204ff.
50. 'Here Be Dragons', *Economist*, 17 April 2010.

51. Ibid.

52. Desai, 'Capitalism by Accident', 38–39.

53. 'The Korean Discount', *Economist*, 11 February 2012.

54. Bloom, et al., 'Why Do Firms in Developing Countries Have Low Productivity?', 619–23.

55. Already referred to by Khanna and Palepu. For a key argument for the importance of political influence, see Bardhan, 'Notes on the Political Economy of India's Tortuous Transition'; or Kali and Sarkar, 'Diversification, Propping and Monitoring'. For allegations of exploitation of the enterprises see Bertrand, Mehta and Mullainathan, 'Ferreting Out Tunneling', 121–48, and for an answer using another set of data and methodology see Siegel and Choudhury, 'A Re-examination of Tunnneling and Business Groups'. These are only illustrative of a larger set of studies in each case, often covering other countries and related issues.

56. Kali and Sarkar, 'Diversification, Propping and Monitoring', 1.

57. Damodaran, *India's New Capitalists*. A more academic formulation is Varshney, 'Two Banks of the Same River?', 225–56.

Afterword

1. Tandon, *The Punjabi Saga*.

2. K.K. Birla, *Brushes with History*, 61; B.K. Birla, *A Rare Legacy*.

3. Benjamin and Rath, 'Modern Indian Business History'.

4. Bhagat, *One Night @ the Call Center*; Bhagat, *The Three Mistakes of My Life*.

5. Sankar, *Chowringhee*.
6. Prindle, *Made in Japan and Other Japanese 'Business Novels'*; Gordon, 'Japanese Business Novels'; Davies, 'The Financial Fiction Genre'.

BIBLIOGRAPHY

Alfaro, Laura and Anusha Chari. 'India Transformed? Insights from the Firm Level 1988-2007'. Paper prepared for presentation at the NCAER-Brookings Policy Forum 2009. New Delhi: 14–15 July 2009. Available online at http://www.ncaer.org/downloads/ipf2009/ipf09_paper_charialfaro.pdf.

Bajranga Lal Kedia v. King-Emperor. All India Reporter 1921. Calcutta, 719.

Banfield, Edward. *The Moral Basis of a Backward Society*. Chicago: Free Press, 1958.

Bardhan, Pranab. 'Notes on the Political Economy of India's Tortuous Transition'. *Economic and Political Weekly* XLIV, no. 49 (5 December 2009).

Barontini, Roberto and Lorenzo Caprio. 'The Effect of Family Control on Firm Value and Performance': Evidence 3 from Continental Europe. 15 May 2005.

Batala, Eric Vincent C. 'Zaibatsu Development in the Philippines: The Ayala Model'. *Southeast Asian Studies* 37, no. 1 (June 1999): 18–49.

Bengal Hurkaru. 10 May 1834. 4–5.

Benjamin, N. and Prabhash Narayana Rath. 'Modern Indian Business History: A Bibliographic Survey'. Available online at www.esocialsciences.com/data/articles/Document1382007210.3797266.pdf.

Bertrand, Marianne and Antoinette Schoar. 'The Role of Family in Family Firms'. *Journal of Economic Perspectives* 20, no. 2 (Spring 2006): 73–96.

Bertrand, Marianne, Paras Mehta and Sendhil Mullainathan. 'Ferreting Out Tunneling: An Application to Indian Business Groups'. *The Quarterly Journal of Economics* 117, no. 1 (February 2002): 121–48.

Bhagat, Chetan. *One Night @ the Call Center*. New Delhi: Rupa and Co., 2005.

———. *The Three Mistakes of My Life: A Story about Business, Cricket and Religion*. New Delhi: Rupa and Co., 2008.

Birla, B.K. *A Rare Legacy: Memoirs of B.K. Birla*. Bombay: Image Incorporated, 1994.

Birla, K.K. *Brushes with History: An Autobiography*. New Delhi: Penguin, 2007.

Birla, Ritu. *Stages of Capitalism: Law, Culture, and Market Governance in Late Colonial India*. Durham, NC: Duke University Press, 2009.

Bloom, Nicholas, Aprajit Mahajan, David McKenzie and John Roberts. 'Why Do Firms in Developing Countries Have Low Productivity?'. *American Economic Review* 100 (2): 619–23.

Cohen, Allan R. 'Tradition, Values and Inter-Role Conflict in Indian Family Business'. Unpublished DBA thesis. Cambridge, MA: Harvard Business School, 1967.

———. *Tradition, Change and Conflict in Indian Family Business*. The Hague: Brill, 1974.

Crabtree, James. 'India's Billionaires Club'. *Financial Times*, 16 November 2012.

Damodaran, Harish. *India's New Capitalists: Case, Business, and Industry in a Modern Nation*. Ranikhet, UP: Permanent Black, 2008.

Das, Gurcharan. *India Unbound*. New York: A.A. Knopf, 2001.

Datta, Kausik. 'Kumar Mangalam: The Biggest Birla'. *Business Standard*, 19 September 2005. Available online at http://www.rediff.com/money/2005/sep/19spec.htm.

Davies, Roy. 'The Financial Fiction Genre: Japanese Business Novels'. 11 October 2004. Available online at http://projects.exeter.ac.uk/RDavies/bankfiction/scifi.html.

Desai, Nitin. 'Capitalism by Accident'. *Economic and Political Weekly* XLVII, no. 35 (1 September 2012): 38–39.

Edwardes, S.M. and Sir James MacNabb Campbell. *The Gazetteer of Bombay City and Island*. Vol. 1. Bombay: Times Press, 1909.

Gazetteer of Bombay Presidency. Vol. IV. Ahmedabad and Bombay, 1879.

Goodwin, Iris. 'How the Rich Stay Rich: Using a Family Trust Company to Secure a Family Fortune'. University of Tennessee Legal Studies Research Paper No. 61. 20 April 2009. Available online at http://ssrn.com/abstract=1392983.

Gordon, Bill. 'Japanese Business Novels'. May 2000. Available online at http://www.bill-gordon.net/papers/busnovel.htm.

Govindarajan, Vijay and Gunjan Bagla. 'Watch Out For India's Consumer Market Pitfalls'. *Harvard Business Review* (19 October 2012). Available online at http://blogs.hbr.org/2012/10/watch-out-for-indias-consumer/.

Hardgrove, Anne. *Community and Public Culture: The Marwaris in Calcutta, c. 1897–1997*. New York: Columbia University Press, 2007.

———. 'Hindi Literature as a Political Space: Marwari Women's Fiction in Calcutta'. *Economic and Political Weekly* (April 1999): 804–06.

————. 'Sati Worship and Marwari Public Identity in India'. *Journal of Asian Studies* 58, no. 3 (August 1999): 723–52.

'Here Be Dragons: The Emerging World Is Teeming with New Business Models'. *Economist*, 17 April 2010.

'High Net Worth Individuals'. *Economist*, 26 June 2010.

Ho, Karen. *Liquidated: An Ethnography of Wall Street*. Durham, NC: Duke University Press, 2009.

Hopkins, E. Washburn. 'Ancient and Modern Hindu Guilds'. In *India: Old and New*, 169–205. New York: Charles Scribner's Sons, 1902.

Hunt, Tristram. *Marx's General: The Revolutionary Life of Friedrich Engels*. New York: Henry Holt and Company, 2009.

'India's Top 100 Richest'. Last accessed 27 June 2010. Available online at www.sophia-ajz.sulekha/blog.post/2009/11/india-s-top-100-richest-52-billionaires-48-millionaires.

Jackson, Stanley. *The Sassoons*. New York: E.P. Dutton, 1968.

Jhunjhunwala, Vishnu Dayal and Arvind Bharadwaj. *Marwaris: Business Culture and Tradition*. Delhi: Kalpaz Publications, 2002.

Kali, Raja and Jayati Sarkar. 'Diversification, Propping and Monitoring: Business Groups, Firm Performance and the Indian Economic Transition'. Working Paper Series No. WP-2005-006. November 2005. Available online at http://www.igidr.ac.in/pdf/publication/WP-2005-006.

Keynes, John Maynard. *The General Theory of Employment, Interest and Money*. London: McMillan and Co., 1936.

Khanna, Tarun and Krishna G. Palepu. 'The Evolution of Concentrated Ownership in India: Broad Patterns and a History of the Indian Software Industry'. In Randall K. Morck, ed., *A History of Corporate Governance Around the World: Business Groups to Professional Managers*, 283–94. Chicago, IL: University of Chicago Press, 2005.

Knowledge@wharton. 'The New "Right-Hand Men": The Growing Role of Women in Indian Family Business'.

5 November 2009. Available online at http://knowledge.wharton.upenn.edu/article/new-right-hand-men-the-growing-role-of-women-in-indian-family-business/.

Krishnan, Shekhar. 'Bombay Cotton: Share Mania in the Colonial City'. Paper presented at the Workshop on the Political Economy of Modern Capitalism, Harvard University Department of History and Harvard Law School. Cambridge, MA: April 2008.

Kudaisya, Medha M. *The Life and Times of G.D. Birla*. New Delhi: Oxford University Press, 2003.

Leahy, Joe. 'Ambani Brothers Agree Peace Deal'. *Financial Times*, 24 May 2010.

Leonard, Karen Isaksen. 'Family Firms in Hyderabad: Gujarati, Goswami, and Marwari Patterns of Adoption, Marriage, and Inheritance'. *Comparative Studies in Society and History* 53, no. 4 (2011): 827–54.

Little, J.H. *The House of Jagatseth*. Calcutta: Calcutta Historical Society, 1967.

McClelland, David. *The Achieving Society*. New York: Free Press, 1961

Milman, Harry A. 'The Marwari: A Study of a Group of Trading Castes'. Unpublished MA thesis. Berkeley, CA: University of California, 1954.

Misra, Maria. *Business, Race, and Politics in British India, c. 1850-1960*. Oxford: Clarendon Press, 1999.

O'Hara, William T. and Peter Mandel. 'The World's Oldest Family Companies: Convincing Evidence that Smaller Firms Usually Outlast Larger Ones'. 2003. Available online at http://www.griequity.com/resources/industryandissues/familybusiness/oldestinworld.html.

Owens, Raymond and Ashis Nandy. *The New Vaishyas*. Bombay: Allied Publishers, 1973.

Parson, Rahul Bjørn. 'The Bazaar and the Bari: Calcutta, the Marwaris, and the World of Hindi Letters'. Available online at http://www.escholarship.org/uc/item/7ng958qz.

Piramal, Gita. *Business Maharajas.* New Delhi: Penguin, 1996.

Porter, Michael E. *Competitive Strategy: Techniques for Analyzing Industries and Competitors.* New York: Free Press, 1998.

Prindle, Tamae K. *Made in Japan and Other Japanese 'Business Novels'.* Armonk, NY: M.E. Sharpe, 1989.

Rahman, Shafi. 'The Big Story: Battles for Billions'. *India Today*, 5 March 2012.

'Rank of Cities on Sanitation 2009-2010: National Urban Sanitation Policy'. Press Information Bureau. May 2010. Available online at pib.nic.in/archieve/others/2010/may/d2010051101.pdf.

Ray, Rajat Kumar. 'Asian Capital in the Age of European Domination: the Rise of the Bazaar, 1800-1914'. *Modern Asian Studies* 29, 3 (July 1995): 449–554.

Rice, A.K. *Productivity and Social Organization: The Ahmedabad Experiment; Technical Innovation, Work Organization and Management.* London: Tavistock Publications, 1958.

Roth, Cecil. *The Sassoon Dynasty.* London: Robert Hale, 1941.

Rudolph, Lloyd and Susanne Rudolph. 'From Landed Class to Middle Class: Rajput Adaptation in Rajasthan'. Available online at http://political-science.uchicago.edu/faculty-articles/Rudophs%20--%20Baviskar.pdf.

Rudolph, Lloyd and Susanne Rudolph. *The Modernity of Tradition: Political Development in India.* Chicago, IL: University of Chicago Press, 1966.

Sanghvi, Vir. *Men of Steel: India's Business Leaders in Candid Conversation with Vir Sanghvi.* New Delhi: Roli Books, 2007.

Sankar. *Chowringhee.* New Delhi: Penguin, 2007.

Saxena, Anand. 'Succession in Indian Business Houses'. 9 November 2009. Available online at http://papers.ssrn.com/sol3/papers.cfm?abstract_id=1502702.

Sharp, Henry. *Good-Bye India.* London: Oxford University Press, 1946.

Siegel, Jordan and Prithviraj Choudhury. 'A Re-examination of Tunneling and Business Groups: New Data and New Methods'. Working Paper 10-072, Harvard Business School.

Singer, Milton. *When a Great Tradition Modernizes: An Anthropological Approach to Indian Civilization*. New York: Praeger, 1972.

Sinha, Jayant and Ashutosh Varshney. 'It is Time for India to Rein in Its Robber Barons'. *Financial Times*, 6 January 2011.

Sinha, N.K. 'Introduction'. In J.H. Little, *The House of Jagatseth*, v–xxiii. Calcutta: Calcutta Historical Society, 1967.

Taleb, Nassim Nicholas. *Antifragile: Things That Gain from Disorder.* New York: Random House, 2014.

Talreja, Aditi. 'Succession in Indian Family Firms: Impact of Successions on Performance of Indian Family Firms'. Honours thesis, Leonard N. Stern School of Business. New York: New York University, May 2007.

Tandon, Prakash. *Punjabi Century, 1857-1947*. New York: Harcourt, Brace & World, 1961.

————. *The Punjabi Saga, 1857-2000: The Monumental Story of Five Generations of a Remarkable Punjabi Family*. New Delhi: Rupa and Co., 2000.

Tewari, S.N. *Business Communities and the Freedom Struggle: A Case History of Rajasthan*. Jaipur: Aalekh Publishers, 1992.

Thakurdas Mundra v. Emperor. All India Reporter 1930. Calcutta, 637. India Cases 128 (Calcutta High Court).

'The Inheritors'. *India Today*, March 2012.

'The Korean Discount: Minority Report'. *Economist*, 11 February 2012.

'The Rise, Fall and Rise of Indian Business Families: Make Way for the Heroes'. Last accessed 15 March 2014. Available online at http://www.businessandeconomy.org/14122006/storyd. asp?sid=641&pageno=19.

'The World's Billionaires'. *Forbes.com*. Available online at http://www.forbes.com/lists/2010/10/billionaires-2010_The-Worlds-Billionaires_Rank.html.

Timberg, Thomas A. *The Marwaris: From Traders to Industrialists*. New Delhi: Vikas, 1978.

Tod, James. *Annals and Antiquities of Rajasthan, or The Central and Western Rajput State of India*. Vol. 2. Calcutta, 1894.

Tripathi, Dwijendra and Jyoti Jumani. *The Concise Oxford History of Indian Business*. New Delhi: Oxford University Press, 2008.

Varshney, Ashutosh .'Two Banks of the Same River? Social Order and Entrepreneurialism in India'. In Partha Chatterjee and Ira Katznelson, eds, *Anxieties of Democracy: Tocquevillean Reflections on India and the United States*. New Delhi: Oxford University Press, 2012.

Wacha, Sir Dinshaw Edulji. *A Financial Chapter in the History of Bombay City*. Bombay: A.J. Combridge and Co., 1910.

Wacziarg, Francis and Aman Nath. *Rajasthan: The Painted Walls of Shekhavati*. London: Croom Helm, 1982.

Weber, Max. *The Religion of India: The Sociology of Hinduism and Buddhism*. New York: Free Press, 1958.

Wikipedia. 'Bhaiband'. Available online at en.wikipedia.org/wiki/Bhaiband.

———. 'Corporate Group'. Available online at http://en.wikipedia.org/wiki/Corporate_group.

———. 'Lohana'. Available online at en.wikipedia.org/wiki/Lohan.

Wiwattanakantang, Yupana. 'Are Japanese Family Firms Successful?'. Research Institute of Economy, Trade and Industry. Available online at http://www.rieti.go.jp/en/projects/cgp/columns/10.html.

Yang, Anand A. *Bazaar India: Markets, Society, and the Colonial State in Bihar*. Berkeley, CA: University of California Press, 1998.

Zaloom, Caitlin. *Out of the Pits: Trader and Technology from Chicago to London*. Chicago: University of Chicago Press, 2006.

INDEX

Introduction by Gurcharan Das

Arthashastra: The Science of Wealth

Thomas R. Trautmann

What is the secret of creating and sustaining wealth?

Ascribed to Kautilya (commonly identified as the prime minister of Chandragupta Maurya) and dating back more than 2000 years, the *Arthashastra* is the world's first manual in political economy. This book is intended to be an introduction to the economic philosophy of the *Arthashastra*, and its relevancy in the present times is indisputable.

The World of the Tamil Merchant: Pioneers of International Trade

Kanakalatha Mukund

How did the Tamil merchant become India's first link to the outside world?

The tale of the Tamil merchant is a fascinating story of the adventure of commerce in the ancient and early medieval period in India. The early medieval period saw an economic structure dominated by the rise of powerful Tamil empires under the Pallava and Chola dynasties. This book marks the many significant ways in which the Tamil merchants impacted the political and economic development of South India.

Introduction by Gurcharan Das

The East India Company: The World's Most Powerful Corporation

Tirthankar Roy

How did the East India Company change the way in which business was conducted in India?

For over 200 years, the East India Company was the largest and most powerful mercantile firm in Britain and Asia. Originally set up to procure Asian goods for British consumers, how and why did a merchant firm end up being an empire builder? This book answers these questions by taking a fresh look at the world of Indian business.

Three Merchants of Bombay: Doing Business in Times of Change

Lakshmi Subramanian

How did the traders of Bombay shape capitalism in India?

Three Merchants of Bombay is the story of three intrepid merchants—Trawadi Arjunji Nathji, Jamsetjee Jeejeebhoy and Premchand Roychand—who traded out of Bombay in the nineteenth century, founding pioneering business empires, a proud milestone in the history of indigenous capitalism in India. This book traces that history and locates it in the greater narrative of the history of economic development in South Asia.

Introduction by Gurcharan Das

The Mouse Merchant: Money in Ancient India
Arshia Sattar

What did ancient Indians think of money?

Even in ancient India, money is always a good thing and everyone wants it. The stories in *The Mouse Merchant*— selected from the Sanskrit universe, from the period of the late *Rig Veda* to the twelfth century—tell us how money was dealt with in everyday life in ancient and medieval Indian society. At the heart of these tales is the merchant. This book gives rare insights into the romance of the ancient seafaring life apart from imparting great wisdom about money.

Caravans: Indian Merchants on the Silk Road
Scott C. Levi

The great adventure of the Multani merchants on the Silk Road to Central Asia

Caravans tells the fascinating story of the thousands of intrepid Multani and Shikarpuri merchants who risked everything to travel great distances and spend years of their lives pursuing their fortunes in foreign lands. The book examines the sophisticated techniques these merchants used to convert a modest amount of merchandise into vast portfolios of trade and also argues that the rising tide of European trade in the Indian Ocean usurped the overland 'Silk Road' trade and pushed Central Asia into economic isolation.